EXPLORING POETRY OF PRESENCE

A COMPANION GUIDE FOR READERS, WRITERS, & WORKSHOP FACILITATORS

GLORIA HEFFERNAN

Foreword by
PHYLLIS COLE-DAI & RUBY R. WILSON

BACK PORCH PRODUCTIONS LLC

ISBN: 978-1-7371055-0-3

For information write to the publisher:
Back Porch Productions LLC, 46855 200th St., Bruce SD 57220-5210.

Visit the author's website: https://gloriaheffernan.wordpress.com

Author photograph credit: Jim Heffernan.

FOREWORD

Sometimes a gift drops on us like a refreshing shower from a blue, cloudless sky, and all we can do is gaze up and wonder, "Where did this come from?" Such is the case with this guidebook.

Last May, as the pandemic was sweeping around the globe, Gloria Heffernan emailed the two of us a thank-you poem for *Poetry of Presence*. One of its stanzas read:

> So if you ever wonder,
> I want to tell you both that you
> are essential workers.
> I want you to know that
> in these dark days when everything has
> Changed, changed utterly,
> one thing that remains is the peace
> I find when I open your book to a random page
> and find exactly the words I need to hear.

—excerpt, "In Case You Ever Wonder"

While Gloria's poem was an unexpected gift in itself, little did we know that the correspondence it initiated would lead to her creation of this resource. We thank Gloria for generously sharing such a storehouse of practical knowledge with the rest of us. *Exploring Poetry of Presence* is bursting with creative ideas on how we can all deepen our use and appreciation of *Poetry of Presence: An Anthology of Mindfulness Poems.*

Are you a reader of poetry? A poet yourself? A classroom teacher? A facilitator of workshops in which you somehow employ poetry? Because Gloria is all of these, you can draw upon this companion guide with confidence. Every suggestion springs from her rich experience, not to mention her expressive, compassionate heart.

Adapt this text to your needs. Experiment. See where it might take you. Why? For joy. For sustenance. And for the sake of an ailing world, which needs the vitality and vision of poetry more than ever.

Phyllis Cole-Dai & Ruby R. Wilson
Editors, *Poetry of Presence*

PREFACE

When Phyllis Cole-Dai and Ruby R. Wilson published *Poetry of Presence* in 2017 (Grayson Books), they could not have imagined the pandemic and social unrest that would unfold just three years later. Nor would they have considered themselves what we now call "essential workers." But as spring and summer of 2020 progressed, I experienced just how essential their work was and continues to be. As Mary Oliver says in "When I am Among the Trees," "I would almost say that they save me, and daily" (44).

I found myself turning to *Poetry of Presence* more and more. It was my antidote to the news. After hours of watching the numbers of cases and casualties soaring, I would turn off the television and open the book to a random page. Always, no matter what page I turned to, I found an invitation to quiet my mind. To be still. To trust.

When I saw how this practice was helping me, I became eager to share it with others. I proposed a course to the Downtown Writers Center at the YMCA in Syracuse, New York. The course was called "Poetry of the Essential: Turning to Poetry in Times of Crisis," which has evolved into the "Poetry of Presence Workshop."

The class, which took place over Zoom, attracted participants from Connecticut, New York, Pennsylvania, and California. The response from participants was overwhelmingly positive. It was a joy and a privilege to facilitate the workshop and to know that it was helping people during such a dark time.

In the meantime, I had written to Phyllis and Ruby, to thank them for *Poetry of Presence*. Through this anthology, they had become my unseen companions during many precious moments of peace since the very first time I opened the book.

I thank Phyllis and Ruby with all my heart.

Gloria Heffernan
Syracuse, New York
January 2021

HOW TO USE THIS BOOK

This book is subtitled *A Companion Guide for Readers, Writers, and Workshop Facilitators.* It isn't intended to be an instruction manual or a textbook. Rather, it celebrates the fact that reading poetry is an active and communal pursuit. It takes us places. It's good to have a companion on the journey, a guide who knows the terrain and can point out the highlights.

The guide can tell you the history, and maybe suggest some alternate routes or sites you might want to visit on your own. Ultimately, as Joy Harjo says in "For Calling the Spirit Back from Wandering the Earth in Its Human Feet," "The heart knows the way" (*Poetry of Presence,* 189).

Your heart knows the way. It knows the value of pausing for a moment to catch your breath. It knows that focus and calm can carry you further than chaos and adrenaline. It knows that mindfulness isn't just the path; it's the vehicle.

The introduction to *Poetry of Presence* is "The Invitation." It opens with this paragraph:

 Some poems are good medicine. They soothe our anxieties and self-doubt, restore our balance, boost our energy and strength, help us cope with stress, or even heal. Such poems we tend to keep, and share. We dog-ear their pages. We copy them down in our journals. We mull them over in times of reflection. We pass them around in book clubs, support groups and classrooms. We send them to loved ones and friends. We read them aloud to mark special days, to observe sacred days, to endure sad days. We utter them like prayers. (17)

This guidebook is for all of us who have accepted that invitation and want to continue on the journey.

The chief intention of this guidebook is to enrich your experience of *Poetry of Presence*. It includes some engaging reading strategies and fifty prompts to stimulate ideas for your own writing. It also includes a workshop curriculum for people who are interested in leading others through the reading and writing process. Every prompt can be a source for journal entries, poems, and discussions.

Allow *Poetry of Presence* to take you places. Let the poems serve as the "good medicine" that the editors of the anthology, Phyllis Cole-Dai and Ruby R. Wilson, prescribed in their initial invitation. As you engage with the poems, let them bring you the peace that comes from mindfulness.

CONTENTS

PART III: FOR WORKSHOP FACILITATORS

PART I: FOR READERS

INTRODUCTION

There is no wrong way to read *Poetry of Presence*. But here are some of the ways I have learned to enjoy it. Let's call them "the multiple R's."

- Random Reading
- Relevant Reading
- Responsive Reading
- Restorative Reading
- Round-Robin Reading
- Relay Reading
- Reading as a Pathway to Writing

RANDOM READING

Random Reading is my favorite way to read *Poetry of Presence*, letting it find me where I am. I often turn to it as I would a trusted friend whom I can always count on to tell me what I need to hear. Like that trusted friend, it never fails.

I began using Random Reading as an intentional practice during the spring of 2020 when I often found myself consumed and sometimes paralyzed by the news. There were days when I sat, transfixed, watching the pandemic numbers rise in the columns on the right-hand side of the screen as CNN scrolled through the daily counts. I felt helpless and, worse yet, useless.

Then, one day in mid-April, I turned off the news and picked up *Poetry of Presence*. It wasn't hard to find. It is usually on top of whatever stack of books I am reading at any given moment. I opened it to a random page, trusting that I would find words that would help me quiet my mind.

I opened to Alice Walker's "I Will Keep Broken Things" (146), a poem I have read many times that always yields rich new insights. I don't know when the tears started streaming down my cheeks. Maybe it was when I read the lines:

Thank you
so much!

I will keep
broken
things.
I will keep
you:

pilgrim
of
sorrow.

I will keep
myself. (148)

To find the words *"Thank you/so much"* in the midst of that brokenness was a revelation. To recognize my own brokenness as a pilgrimage through this time of crisis was a healing testament.

I have consciously engaged in the practice of Random Reading many times since then. If it sounds like silly superstition, it isn't. I don't profess that the book has some mysterious psychic power. It is more like a well-stocked pantry that I can turn to when I am hungry, knowing that when I need nourishment, I can reach in and be fed. It never fails to satisfy.

RELEVANT READING

Relevant Reading has to do with where you are right now and what you might need in this moment. Relevant Reading is the active pursuit of a particular poem or theme. It is a response to a specific moment or need: the pain of anxiety or grief, awe at the sight of a brilliant sunset, or wonder at the song of an unseen bird. These are all moments when you might seek out a poem that is relevant to that emotion or experience.

When I am going through a turbulent or difficult time, I know that I will find perseverance and peace in Judy Sorum Brown's "Trough" (128). If I am feeling stuck in my own writing, I can easily find the dog-eared and annotated "How to Be a Poet" by Wendell Berry (103), which reminds me to quiet myself and "Accept what comes from silence." When I need to calm down, I need look no further than Pablo Neruda's "Keeping quiet" (104). I don't even need to consult the Contents anymore. I know where to find these poems, and truth be told, I have turned to these pages so often, the book frequently opens to them of its own accord. The spine naturally bends after years of practice. (Yes, reading can be a form of yoga!)

If you are looking for one of these "relevant" poems, and don't already know where to find it, I have created a Subject Index to help.

RESPONSIVE READING

Responsive Reading is done with a journal at hand. Read a poem and then reflect on it in your journal for five minutes. Keeping your journal entry brief makes it feel less like a chore and invites quick, clear responses. As you develop the practice, it helps you to home in on the essence of your response.

A variation on this approach is to choose a poem and spend time with it over a period of days. Read the same piece every day for a week writing a five-minute reflection each time. At the end of the week, read the entries as a single document. What does it reveal?

REPETITIVE READING

Repetitive reading is like studying a poem through a prism. It offers multiple viewpoints when viewed from different angles.

Choose a poem (or let it choose you) and read it aloud once. Savor it for a minute or two. Then read it again, consciously slowing your pace. Pause after reading it and allow yourself to rest in the words. Read it a third time, but now read it silently. Notice what images call your attention. Does your focus change from one reading to the next? Does the feeling change when you transition from reading aloud to reading silently? Which do you prefer? Why?

Journal about the poem for five minutes. Again, it is helpful to keep the journaling brief as it helps you to focus on the essentials. What is the poem saying to you right now? Observe how each successive reading draws you farther into the poem.

RESTORATIVE READING

Restorative Reading is like Restorative Yoga. It invites you to relax, breathe deeply, stretch, and rest in the artistry of the poems. It is a truly mindful approach to slowly savoring and experiencing every word.

Restorative Reading can help you unwind before going to sleep. Try keeping the anthology on your nightstand. Spend a few moments reading a poem as you prepare to drift off to sleep. It can offer a contemplative break that will quiet the anxious end-of-the-day thoughts that often make sleep difficult to achieve. It might even lead to sweeter dreams!

ROUND-ROBIN READING

Round-Robin Reading is a little bit like a potluck dinner. It is a feast of favorite poems enjoyed in a social setting. Participants bring a selection of poems and take turns reading them aloud. Each person reads one poem per round. The number of poems depends on the size of the group and the amount of time allotted. There is no discussion between poems. It is simply an ongoing process of reading and listening. There is no need to worry if more than one person picks the same poem; it is always different coming from another voice.

Round-Robin Readings aren't just for classes and workshops. They are an engaging way to enjoy a social gathering with friends who share your love of poetry. It can even be done as a virtual get-together over Zoom if you are not able to be together in person.

RELAY READING

Relay Reading is another form of social engagement through poetry. To engage in Relay Reading, a pair of readers chooses a poem and reads it in relay fashion. Reader A reads the first line, Reader B reads the second line, and the two alternate until the poem is finished. Then the two readers switch roles. Now B reads the first and A reads the second. The poem is then read a third time in unison. This approach allows the participants to embody the words in a way that fosters a more intimate relationship with the poem.

READING AS A PATHWAY TO WRITING

After spending many hours reading *Poetry of Presence*, you may feel inspired to try writing your own poems. If so, have no fear. The rest of this book is for you too. In the upcoming pages, you will find 50 writing prompts inspired by various works in the anthology.

The truth is, we are all poets. It's just that some of us haven't activated the account yet. I hope you will do that now in mindful appreciation and celebration of your own voice.

PART II: FOR WRITERS

This section of *Exploring Poetry of Presence* features fifty prompts to inspire your own writing. Whether you are a beginner or an experienced writer, prompts are a highly effective tool for generating new ideas, often with surprising results.

Each prompt offers an invitation to write a poem on a specific theme or topic related to the works in *Poetry of Presence*. The prompt is followed by a brief list of "Poems for Inspiration" selected from the anthology. The selected poems demonstrate how other poets have written about the theme addressed in the prompt. I urge you to spend time contemplating those poems both for inspiration and to appreciate the wide variety of ways in which a prompt may be interpreted.

50 WRITING PROMPTS

Before you begin working with these fifty prompts, I ask you to keep a few core principles in mind:

1. *Prompts are simply invitations to exploration.* Please come back to this phrase again and again as you work.

2. *Prompts are effective for both journaling and writing poems.* Don't feel pressured to produce a poem in response to every prompt. It will become burdensome and rob you of the joy of mindful engagement in the writing process.

3. *Prompts are not assignments.* I have often heard people apologize in workshops for writing a marvelous poem that bears little resemblance to the prompt. To those people I say, "Congratulations! You have used the prompt well!"

4. *Prompts are environmentally friendly.* They are at their best when recycled and reused! I love to go back to a prompt months after I have first used it. The same prompt can inspire an entirely new poem.

5. *Prompts are not mirrors.* Sample poems are provided to illustrate the variety of ways in which a prompt can be explored. Please don't let these examples intimidate you. Just let them help you write your own poems in your own unique voice. You are the only one who can.

6. *Prompts require no maps or GPS units.* You never really want to know where you are going when you set out to write a poem. Allow yourself to be surprised. Turn off that main road, even (or especially) if you don't know where it will take you. You are cordially invited to get lost in any prompt.

7. *"Prompt" does not suggest a timetable.* The word might make you think that if you're not prompt, you're too late. But that's not the case. A prompt is a great way to get started on a poem, but you must remember that the poem will arrive in its own good time. Just think of the last time you were waiting for a plane. Chances are it wasn't prompt. (Are they ever?) But ultimately, you arrived at your destination … no matter how long it took to get there!

8. *Prompts are biodegradable.* Sometimes writers express frustration when their response to a prompt doesn't yield a poem they consider good enough. I have even heard them refer to their own work as "garbage." Let me assure you: No prompt has ever produced garbage. It is all organic. If you are not happy with it, feel free to toss it into the compost heap. Let it nourish and fertilize the next crop of poems. Remember that nothing is wasted as long as you keep making use of it.

9. *Prompts are portable.* Take an idea with you wherever you go. You can always carry the seeds of inspiration. Are you thinking about prompt #47 but you don't feel like sitting at your desk? No problem! Take it outside!

10. *Prompts are simply invitations to exploration.* See, I told you to keep

coming back to this phrase as you work with the following prompts. Sometimes we just need a little reminder.

1

WRITE A RESPONSE POEM

Response poems are a rewarding way of conversing with a poem you love. They can also serve as a tribute to a poet whose work you admire.

There are numerous ways to approach the response poem:

- You might respond to a poem directly, as if you were responding to a letter from the poet.

- You might begin with an epigraph, using a quote from the source poem. The epigraph stands alone in italics under the title and includes the author's name. This quote becomes the focus of your new poem.

- You might write a thank you letter in the form of a poem to a poet whose work inspires you.

- You might write a poem that echoes the style of another but addresses a different subject, as Ruby R. Wilson does in "Another Ocean" (161). This piece is written in the style of Mary Oliver, whose poems about the seashore in

Massachusetts inspired Wilson's tribute to the prairie in her home state, South Dakota. Wilson acknowledges Oliver's influence with a note after the title.

Choose one of these methods and write a poem in response to a piece in *Poetry of Presence*.

POEMS FOR INSPIRATION:

Note: Page numbers under "Poems for Inspiration" in all writing prompts refer to *Poetry of Presence.*

- "Sunday Afternoon," Nancy Ann Schaefer, 43.
- "Another Ocean," Ruby R. Wilson, 161.

2

THRESHOLDS: ENTERING A MINDFUL STATE

Mindfulness has no membership dues or equipment and requires no special training. All it requires is a choice.

When entering a mindful state, we cross a threshold from the chaotic to the contemplative. Sometimes we have to seek out that threshold. Sometimes we stumble over it into a quiet place of attention and focus.

Thresholds are all around us: the change of seasons, dawn, dusk, coming home from a long day at work, waking up from a restful sleep. Any of these passages can serve as a threshold into mindful presence.

Write a poem about a time when you crossed a threshold. What was it that caught your attention? How did it engage your senses? Did you feel your breathing slow down? Did your posture change? How did crossing the threshold change your perspective?

POEMS FOR INSPIRATION:

- "Bali Hai Calls Mama," Marilyn Nelson, 34.
- "Thinking," Danusha Laméris, 47.

- "Still Life at Dusk," Rosemerry Wahtola Trommer, 65.
- "Getting Up Early," Anne Porter, 66.
- "Surprised by Evening," Robert Bly, 126.
- "the door," Miroslav Holub (translation by Ian and Jarmila Milner et al.), 139.
- "Entrance," Rainer Maria Rilke (translation by Dana Gioia), 162.
- "In Early Evening," Kirsten Dierking, 196.

(Used in Week 1 Workshop, page 143 in this guide)

3

BLESSINGS AND GRATITUDE IN TIMES OF STRESS

In the midst of tremendous stress, how do we maintain our equilibrium and peace of mind? One source is gratitude. Writing a poem that expresses gratitude can draw your attention away from the things that are troubling you. It shifts your attention and redirects your energy.

Write a poem in the form of a gratitude list. Include everything/everyone that comes to mind. Resist the temptation to explain anything. Let the associations surprise you. Use all your senses so that you can engage all of your reader's senses. Let gratitude drive the poem.

After you have written your list poem, choose a particular item from the list and write a poem focusing on why you are grateful for it. Explore the many reasons for your gratitude. Drill down into the deepest level of detail you can reach. Imagine the object of your gratitude as a giant peony and you are the ant exploring every petal. This project helps guide you away from the negative by directing your attention to something gratifying.

* * *

POEMS FOR INSPIRATION:

- "Praise Song," Barbara Crooker, 45.
- "A Poem for My Daughter," Teddy Macker, 113.
- "Gracias/Grace," Rafael Jesús González, 118.
- "I Will Keep Broken Things," Alice Walker, 146..

4

WALKING MEDITATIONS

We often think of meditation as something that is done while sitting still in a quiet room. But that is by no means the only way to do it. Walking also offers pathways to contemplation.

Many of the selections in *Poetry of Presence* are invitations to explore a wide variety of paths. As Julia Fehrenbacher says in "The Cure for It All":

> Go gently today, don't hurry
> or think about the next thing. Walk
> with the quiet trees. (40)

Where might you walk today? Is there a path you want to follow? Is there some new trail you have yet to explore? Take a lesson from Mary Oliver, who described her practice of taking long walks every morning. She always carried a pad and pencil in her pocket to capture whatever images came to mind.

Read the following selections from *Poetry of Presence*, then go for a walk. After you have been walking for 20 minutes, find a place to sit down. Observe your surroundings. Write five images that describe where you are sitting. Don't try to write a poem right now. Just collect the images. What do you see? Hear? Feel? Smell? How does it feel to carry your body into the wind or through the summer heat? After you have compiled the list, put your notebook back in your pocket and keep walking.

When you return home, use the list to help you write a poem that recreates your walk. Invite your reader to explore the path with you.

POEMS FOR INSPIRATION:

- "The Cure for It All," Julia Fehrenbacher, 40.
- "Under Ideal Conditions," Al Zolynas, 60.
- "The Bare Arms of Trees," John Tagliabue, 78.
- "I Am Going to Start Living Like a Mystic," Edward Hirsch, 108.
- "Winter Grace," Patricia Fargnoli, 157.
- "Walking a Field into Evening," Larry Smith, 164.
- "Fog," Twyla M. Hansen, 179.

5

THE PRESENCE OF LOVE

What makes a great love poem?

Perhaps it is easier to answer the question, what makes a really bad love poem? Bad love poems rely on sentimentality, generality, and cliché. Few subjects are more difficult to convey, but the following poems from *Poetry of Presence* illustrate what is best in love poems.

These works focus on concrete details to convey this profound emotion. Some of the most moving love poems don't even use the word love. They bring us into the presence of love by evoking the beloved in a way that makes the reader love, too.

The love poems in this collection are focused on the mindful expression of love in a myriad of forms: love of family, love of freedom, love of nature, love of self, romantic love. They rely on vivid detail, clarity, and immediacy. They don't fall into the trap of sentimentality or self-indulgence. They evoke the feelings of joy and pain, hope and fear. In short, they honor love by depicting its rich complexity.

After reading the poems below, try writing a 14-line love poem in which the word "love" does not appear. Keep it to 14 lines, the length of a traditional sonnet, to heighten the language. By keeping it brief, you don't have any lines to waste!

POEMS FOR INSPIRATION:

- "Untitled (The Guest is inside you)," Kabir (translation by Robert Bly), 52.
- "Take Love for Granted," Jack Ridl, 53.
- "Love After Love," Derek Walcott, 55.
- "Late Fragment," Raymond Carver, 120.
- "Sweet Darkness," David Whyte, 152.
- "Companion for Life," Hafiz (translation by Daniel Ladinsky), 186.
- "To Have Without Holding," Marge Piercy, 188.

6

WHAT COMES FROM SILENCE

In "Winter Grace" Patricia Fargnoli asserts, "truth is found in silence" (157). This idea is echoed in Wendell Berry's "How to Be a Poet," in which he tells the aspiring writer to "accept what comes from silence/Make the best you can of it" (103).

For many of us, silence is hard to come by in our plugged-in, high-volume world. Where do you go to find silence? Does silence relax you or does it create anxiety?

Find a quiet place and spend some time in silence. You may want to use headphones to eliminate any distractions.

Write a poem about your experience. What truth do you find there?

POEMS FOR INSPIRATION:

- "Lakol Wicoun," Lydia Whirlwind Soldier, 72.
- "Visiting Mountains," Ted Kooser, 73.
- "How to Be a Poet," Wendell Berry, 103.
- "Keeping quiet," Pablo Neruda, 104.

- "Winter Grace," Patricia Fargnoli, 157.
- "Trees," Howard Nemerov, 174.
- "Fog," Twyla M. Hansen, 179.
- "In Early Evening," Kirsten Dierking, 196.

(Used in Week 8 Workshop, page 153 of this guide)

7

A SENSE OF PLACE

We all have a place that holds a special meaning for us. Perhaps it's a national park you visited on vacation ... perhaps a special room in your childhood home ... perhaps the school supply aisle at Target in September. Whatever the place, it is tempting to imagine it through the sense of sight. What does it look like? What are the colors you associate with it?

But this prompt asks you to go beyond the sense of sight to engage the other senses. What does this place sound like? What are the smells and textures? What tastes do you associate with it?

Seamus Heaney's "Postscript" takes the reader to "County Clare, along the Flaggy Shore." He describes the place in rich visual detail, but he doesn't stop there. He creates a physical sensation of the wind blowing and the ocean churning. The poem engages multiple senses, and by the end we are with the narrator in a place that can "catch the heart off guard and blow it open" (101).

Imagine yourself in a special place and recreate it through sound, smell, touch and feel. By exploring the place through multiple senses, you will have access to a wider variety of images that will help bring that place to life. Ask yourself what makes this place unlike any other.

POEMS FOR INSPIRATION:

- "Lie Down," Nancy Paddock, 32.
- "Under Ideal Conditions," Al Zolynas, 60.
- "Visiting Mountains," Ted Kooser, 73.
- "Stone," Danusha Laméris, 91.
- "Postscript," Seamus Heaney, 101.
- "Flowering," Linda Buckmaster, 133.

8

ON FACING DEATH

As I write this prompt, over 500,000 Americans have died of Covid-19. For those who mourn them, death feels anything but poetic. Yet for centuries, people have turned to poets for healing and comfort in times of profound loss.

In *Poetry of Presence*, several poems invite us to consider death from a mindful perspective. These poems seek to express the inexpressible and to provide comfort and courage as we contemplate our own death or that of others.

Sometimes writing a poem or a journal entry can help guide us through the fear of death. Such writing can help us acknowledge the grief, curse the pain, celebrate the memory of the loved one, or do all of those things simultaneously.

I won't presume to suggest a prompt for writing about something so intensely personal. Instead, I simply invite you to read the following poems and find what comfort you can in them. If you feel moved to write something in response, I wish you peace in the words that find their way from your heart to the page.

* * *

POEMS FOR INSPIRATION:

- "Lessons from Darkness," Anita Barrows, 46.
- "Prayer for the Dead," Stuart Kestenbaum, 61.
- "a song with no end," Charles Bukowski, 62.
- "Learning from Trees," Grace Butcher, 124.
- "Savasana: Corpse Pose," Marianne Murphy Zarzana, 125.
- "Surprised by Evening," Robert Bly, 126.
- "The Last Things I'll Remember," Joyce Sutphen, 172.
- "Bedside Manners," Christopher Wiseman, 187.

9

IT'S A BIRD! IT'S A POEM!

Birds are some of nature's greatest super-heroes. The flight of birds has drawn our attention since the first human looked up to the sky. The myth of Daedalus and Icarus has inspired dozens of poems and paintings that speak to our desire to imitate the birds, while reminding us of our inability to do so.

Bird watchers know that studying our feathered friends in their natural habitat requires mindfulness. To learn the songs of different birds requires attention to detail. To wait for a sighting requires patience. Just like the practice of mindfulness in every dimension of our lives, the payoff can be magnificent.

How do you feel when you catch a glimpse of a cardinal resting on a snow-covered branch? Or when a blue jay lifts its wings like a stained-glass window taking flight? Or when you hear the powerful song of a tiny wren? Perhaps it is the fleeting nature of our relationship with birds that makes them so irresistible and inspiring. Perhaps it is our wistful appreciation of their freedom that calls us to pause whatever we are doing and look up when they fly past.

Read the following poems from *Poetry of Presence* and spend some time in the company of birds. Sit in the park and listen. Sit by a window and watch. Or sit at your desk and remember. Wherever you are, contemplate a bird and write a poem about it.

POEMS FOR INSPIRATION:

- "Blackbirds," Julie Cadwallader Staub, 50.
- "Longing," Julie Cadwallader Staub, 63.
- "The Owl Cries at Night," Freya Manfred, 81.
- "This Day," Jimmy Santiago Baca, 84.
- "One Heart," Li-Young Lee, 93.
- "Blue Herons," Twyla M. Hansen, 166.

10

OUR TEACHERS, THE TREES

In "The Quiet Listeners," Laura Foley urges, "Go into the woods/and tell your story/to the trees" (48). The poem offers a glimpse into the intimate relationship between trees and human beings. They are our confidantes, should we recognize them as such.

Poetry of Presence offers a rich variety of poems that celebrate not only the beauty of trees but our spiritual connection to them, and the lessons they have to teach us about the cycles of life, stability, and hope.

Try writing a poem about trees from an unconventional point of view. Are you drawn to a particular tree in your neighborhood or backyard? What makes it special? How does it change with the light? What does it sound like? What story does it want to tell?

POEMS FOR INSPIRATION:

- "Ancient Language," Hannah Stephenson, 29.
- "When I Am Among the Trees," Mary Oliver, 44.
- "The Quiet Listeners," Laura Foley, 48.
- "Lost," David Wagoner, 49.

- "The Offering," Laura Foley, 77.
- "The Bare Arms of Trees," John Tagliabue, 78.
- "Learning from Trees," Grace Butcher, 124.
- "The Moment," Margaret Atwood, 134.
- "Sometimes I Am Startled Out of Myself," Barbara Crooker, 165.
- "Trees," Howard Nemerov, 174.
- "What Else," Carolyn Locke, 183.

11

INSTRUCTIONS FOR LIVING

Do you sometimes wish that life came with a user's manual? Do you find that you can't resist the self-help aisle of your local bookstore because you want to find that one sure-fire guide to getting it right? Or maybe you have all the answers (not likely, but let's just say) and you want to tell the world how it's done.

Write your own "How-To" poem offering instructions for some action or situation. Let each stanza start with a clear declarative statement, and then flesh it out in more poetic terms. Try addressing the reader directly as "you" to give the poem a conversational tone.

The following examples from *Poetry of Presence* offer a wide range of topics and demonstrate the versatility of this style.

POEMS FOR INSPIRATION:

- "On How to Pick and Eat Poems," Phyllis Cole-Dai, 21.
- "A Community of the Spirit," Rumi (translation by Coleman Barks), 27.
- "The Cure for It All," Julia Fehrenbacher, 40.
- "The Quiet Listeners," Laura Foley, 48.

- "Lost," David Wagoner, 49.
- "Take Love for Granted," Jack Ridl, 53.
- "Instructions," Sheri Hostetler, 90.
- "Flowering," Linda Buckmaster, 133.
- "Wage Peace," Judyth Hill, 182.
- "For Calling the Spirit Back from Wandering the Earth in Its Human Feet," Joy Harjo, 189.

(Used in Week 5 Workshop, page 150 of this guide)

12

THE DIGNITY OF WORK

In the wake of the Covid-19 pandemic, we have been reminded of the inherent dignity of work. First responders, nurses, doctors, supermarket clerks, bus drivers, schoolteachers, postal workers ... the list is endless, and it reminds us that everyone is essential. We each have something important to contribute.

Poetry of Presence includes several poems that celebrate both the work and the people who do it, be they parents, teachers, boatbuilders, factory workers, or gardeners.

Spend some time with the following poems and notice how the poets describe each job with respect. Then write a poem about work: yours or someone else's. If you write a poem appreciating another person's work, you get extra points if you give it with them!

POEMS FOR INSPIRATION:

- "Evening Star," Charles Goodrich, 97.
- "When I Taught Her How to Tie Her Shoes," Penny Harter, 107.

- "Twilight," Louise Glück, 143.
- "My Father at the Piano," Mary O'Connor, 159.
- "Wooden Boats" Judy Sorum Brown, 168.
- "Putting in a Window," John Brantingham, 169.
- "An Observation," May Sarton, 181.

13

POEMS FOR THE JOURNEY

Imagine you are preparing for a long trip. Your suitcase is open before you, but instead of clothes and toiletries, you are trying to pack the lessons, stories, poems and prayers that you want to carry with you. What are the essentials that you need to carry? Where will you take them? Where will they take you?

Write a poem about something you must have with you on your personal journey. It doesn't have to be a literal object. It can be a memory or a belief or the lucky pebble you picked up on a hike in the mountains. Describe it in detail as you consider what makes it essential and why you won't leave home without it.

POEMS FOR INSPIRATION:

- "Instructions," Sheri Hostetler, 90.
- "You Are There," Erica Jong, 123.
- "Instructions for the Journey," Pat Schneider, 144.
- "Journey," Linda Hogan, 194.
- "On Pilgrimage," Czelaw Milosz, 195.
- "blessing the boats," Lucille Clifton, 198.

14

PARADISE FOUND

We often think paradise is a place we have to travel to, or something we have to wait to experience in the afterlife. But sometimes paradise is sitting on the couch with a cup of tea and watching the blue jays in the maple tree outside the window.

Spend some time thinking about your definition of paradise. How do you create it in your life? Where have you found it? Write a poem that will take your reader there.

POEMS FOR INSPIRATION:

- "The Bright Field," R. S. Thomas, 150.
- "Another Ocean," Ruby R. Wilson, 161.
- "Walking a Field into Evening," Larry Smith, 164.
- "The Last Things I'll Remember," Joyce Sutphen, 172.
- "On Pilgrimage," Czeslaw Milosz, 195.

15

OUR ANIMAL FAMILY

We have much to learn from animals. Freya Manfred's "The Owl Cries at Night" (81) is an expression of awe at the extraordinary creatures with whom we inhabit this planet, many of whom we never even see. As Manfred contemplates all we can learn from animals, she marvels at the mysteries of nature.

What have you learned from animals? Whether your family pet, the elephant that trumpeted a greeting to you at the zoo, or the squirrel flickering its tail while racing through the trees, animals communicate with us all the time.

Write a poem about an encounter with an animal, real or imagined. What did you learn about the animal and yourself? Focus on specific details and avoid sentimentality. Recall the physical space surrounding the encounter, the time of year, the sounds and smells. If you were afraid, don't say so. Instead describe the way your heart raced or your hands shook. If you were enthralled, describe the physical sensations evoked by the emotion.

* * *

POEMS FOR INSPIRATION:

- "Longing," Julie Cadwallader Staub, 63.
- "A Brief Détente," Rosemerry Wahtola Trommer, 74.
- "The Owl Cries at Night," Freya Manfred, 81.
- "Saint Francis and the Sow," Galway Kinnell, 96.
- "Earthworms," Lynn Ungar, 112.
- "Savasana: Corpse Pose," Marianne Murphy Zarzana, 125.

KEEP, TOSS, GIVE AWAY

Imagine you are planning a garage sale to get rid of all the clutter in your life. How will you choose what to keep, what to toss, what to give away, and what to sell?

Take an inventory of the "stuff" in your home. What are the essentials? What would wind up on the curb? What would you do with that thing you thought you could never part with? What would your space feel like after removing the unessential?

Now take the prompt one step further. What are the memories or emotional baggage that you wish to sort? What would your spiritual space feel like if you tossed the toxic emotions you are holding on to? How would you dispose of the fears and resentments that are cluttering your psychic closet? What are the joys that might serve you better if you gave them away?

Write a poem exploring any or all these questions.

POEMS FOR INSPIRATION:

- "Sifter," Naomi Shihab Nye, 30.
- "The Patience of Ordinary Things," Pat Schneider, 33.

- "In the Middle," Barbara Crooker, 58.
- "Burning the Journals," Robyn Sarah, 132.
- "Meeting the Light Completely," Jane Hirshfield, 140.
- "Plate," Al Zolynas, 145.
- "I Will Keep Broken Things," Alice Walker, 146.
- "On Pain," Kahlil Gibran, 184.

17

WAVES OF WISDOM

Human beings have an endless fascination with bodies of water: the waves, the vastness, and the unpredictability, as well as the peace or trepidation they can inspire.

Since we are 80% water, we might say that the oceans and rivers are literally our element. Water is an extension of ourselves. We look to it for cleansing, for refreshment, for life itself.

Immerse yourself in the following selections from *Poetry of Presence*. Let these poems evoke your own relationship with the water. Can you recall the first time you saw an ocean, lake, or river that filled you with awe? How do you feel when you look out at a calm sea? What do you see when you stand on the prow of a ship or when you paddle a canoe? What does the water say to you? What do you want to say to the water?

Write a poem about a body of water. Speak to it directly, addressing it as "you." Tell the water why you love or fear it. Listen for its reply.

* * *

POEMS FOR INSPIRATION:

- "Rain on Water," Freya Manfred, 127.
- "Trough," Judy Sorum Brown, 128.
- "Seas," Juan Ramón Jiménez (translation by Robert Bly), 197.
- "blessing the boats," Lucille Clifton, 198.

18

PLAY WITH YOUR FOOD

What could be more poetic than biting into a perfect peach with the juice trickling down your chin?

Describing the qualities of food can be a delectable exercise in mindfulness. Consider the smell, texture, cooking process, how it looks on the plate. Using food as a metaphor can remind us of the importance of taking in what nourishes us.

Write a poem celebrating your favorite food. Serve it up to your reader in delicious detail. Set the scene. When did you first taste it? Who else was present? Who prepared it? Engage all the senses.

POEMS FOR INSPIRATION:

- "On How to Pick and Eat Poems," Phyllis Cole-Dai, 21.
- "Meditation on a Grapefruit," Craig Arnold, 39.
- "Love After Love," Derek Walcott, 55.
- "Rutabaga," Laura Grace Weldon, 141.
- "In Plowboy's Produce Market," Donna Hilbert, 177.
- "Smart Cookie," Richard Schiffman, 199.

THE PARADOX OF JOY

In a world torn by crises, joy can seem like an act of disloyalty or denial. We may ask ourselves, "What right do I have to feel joy in a world where suffering runs rampant in the form of hunger, disease, poverty, and injustice?"

How do we balance the suffering of the world with our own experience of joy? The following selections from *Poetry of Presence* explore these questions through the lens of mindfulness. They invite us to be fully present, and to notice what Rosemerry Wahtola Trommer describes as "the path toward joy" (149).

Write a poem about a moment or encounter in which you experience joy. Provide specific details and images. Rather than describing joy, deliver it to your readers in ways they can experience with you.

POEMS FOR INSPIRATION:

- "The Word," Tony Hoagland, 41.
- "Untitled (The Guest is inside you)," Kabir (translation by Robert Bly), 52.

- "This Day," Jimmy Santiago Baca, 84.
- "Mind Wanting More," Holly J. Hughes, 89.
- "One's Ship Comes In," Joe Paddock, 129.
- "Then too there is this," J. Allyn Rosser, 130.
- "The Way It Is," Rosemerry Wahtola Trommer, 149.
- "The Good News," Thich Nhat Hanh, 151.

(Used in Week 4 Workshop, page 149 of this guide)

20

PRESENCE IN THE FACE OF GRIEF

Albert Huffstickler's "The Cure" lays bare the pain of grief in terms that are both uncompromising and hopeful:

> let the pain be pain,
> not in the hope that it will vanish
> but in the faith that it will fit in ... (155)

Achieving that level of acceptance is an arduous task. It requires attention and presence in the face of an emotion we might prefer to avoid. Through mindfulness, we can look at the process of grieving through multiple lenses, including gratitude for the life that is mourned; attention to memory; and peaceful coexistence with the pain.

Poetry can provide an avenue for coping with sorrow. Is there a grief about which you want to write? Spend some time journaling before you attempt to write a poem. Start from where you are. It may be raw and painful. It may come out in a rush of words that you didn't know you were holding back. Just keep writing until you feel like you have gone as far as you want to go.

When you are ready to begin crafting the journal entry into a poem, choose a particular image or detail that you want to explore more fully. Write a short poem about it. The next day, choose another image or detail. Write another short poem about a specific dimension of your experience. By keeping these initial poems brief and focused, you will be less likely to become overwhelmed by the emotions. Eventually, you may want to develop these into longer poems. In the beginning, just give yourself time to "let the pain be pain," as Huffstickler suggests.

POEMS FOR INSPIRATION:

- "Prayer for the Dead," Stuart Kestenbaum, 61.
- "For the Sake of Strangers," Dorianne Laux, 153.
- "The Thing Is," Ellen Bass, 154.
- "The Cure," Albert Huffstickler, 155.
- "On Pain," Kahlil Gibran, 184.

21

AN ODE TO THE UNEXPECTED

An ode is a lyric poem addressed to a particular thing or person, usually as a way to honor, praise or express our gratitude for it. There are countless odes in the poetic canon: odes to spring, to the beloved, to mothers, to a Grecian urn ... you name it. But what about the things we might ordinarily overlook? How might you write a non-traditional ode such as an ode to the dishwasher? Or an ode to the kitchen sink when the dishwasher is broken?

Write an ode to something you might take for granted but really appreciate when you take the time to think about it. It can be serious or funny or seriously funny. The object of this prompt is to be creative in the expression of gratitude and praise. Be as outlandish as you wish, but above all, be surprising!

POEMS FOR INSPIRATION:

- "Sifter," by Naomi Shihab Nye, 30.
- "Meditation on a Grapefruit," Craig Arnold, 39.
- "Love for Other Things," Tom Hennen, 76.
- "Earthworms," Lynn Ungar, 112.

POEMS FROM THE EXPRESS LINE

Never underestimate the power of a short poem. These small gems often focus on a very clear image that stays with the reader long after the book is closed.

Write a short poem of no more than eight lines. Focus on one specific image. Think of the way a fireworks display shoots one intense volley into the air that opens up into countless sparks and colors. It begins with a tightly concentrated kernel of power.

You can also apply this prompt to the revision process. If you have a poem that you have been struggling to revise, try cutting it down to eight lines. The process of selecting what to eliminate will help you sharpen your focus. Michelangelo was known to look at a block of marble and chip away at the stone until the statue within was revealed. Where can you use your hammer and chisel to reveal what lies within the poem by clearing away the excess?

POEMS FOR INSPIRATION:

- "Brotherhood," Octavio Paz (translation by Eliot Weinberger), 59.

- "Fluent," John O'Donohue, 82.
- "One Heart," Li-Young Lee, 93.
- "Late Fragment," Raymond Carver, 120.
- "Zazen on Ching-t'ing Mountain," Li-Po (translation by Sam Hamill), 122.
- "Plate," Al Zolynas, 145.
- "No More Same Old Silly Love Songs," Neil Carpathios, 180.
- "Seas," Juan Ramón Jiménez (translation by Robert Bly), 197.

MEDITATIONS ON NOW

Phyllis Cole-Dai's "On How to Pick and Eat Poems," begins with a clear instruction: "Stop whatever it is you're doing" (21).

When you stop what you are doing, you can begin to notice everything around you at this precise moment: the sound of rain slapping the windows, the hum of the refrigerator, the smell of coffee brewing, the rhythmic breathing of the dog lying on the rug next to your desk.

So, take a few minutes to just stop what you are doing and notice everything. You may find that doing nothing for five minutes is hard work, but the results can be very rewarding.

After five minutes have passed, write a poem that captures the experience of doing nothing in this particular place, at this particular time. What did you notice? How did you feel?

POEMS FOR INSPIRATION:

- "The Way It Is," Lynn Ungar, 31.
- "Lost," David Wagoner, 49.
- "This Morning," David Budbill, 57.

- "A Momentary Creed," W. S. Merwin, 87.
- "Zazen on Ching-t'ing Mountain," Li Po (translation by Sam Hamill), 122.
- "Burning the Journals," Robyn Sarah, 132.
- "Instructions for the Journey," Pat Schneider, 144.
- "The Moment," Marie Howe, 178.

2 4

UNDOINGS

Do you keep a to-do list? Or does it keep you? Is it a scoreboard on which you are always falling behind?

Try a different take on the to-do list. Start with the phrase, "Today I won't…" For example, today I won't worry about getting everything done perfectly. Today I won't be in a constant hurry. Today I won't focus on things I can't control.

Observe how saying no creates space for the authentic yes.

Write the list as a journal entry. Don't try to make it a poem yet.

Put the list away and look at it again tomorrow. Then write a poem about what you didn't do, and how it made a difference.

Poems for inspiration:

- "Bali Hai Calls Mama," Marilyn Nelson, 34.
- "The Word," Tony Hoagland, 41.
- "Thinking," Danusha Laméris, 47.
- "Then too there is this," J. Allyn Rosser, 130.
- "The Moment," Marie Howe, 178.

GETTING OUT OF OUR OWN WAY

In "Because even the word *obstacle* is an obstacle," Alison Luterman issues a challenging invitation: "Try to love everything that gets in your way" (88). Her litany of examples has a common thread: the thing that most frequently gets in our way is our limited perception of the things that get in our way.

Read the following selections from *Poetry of Presence* and recall a moment when you got in your own way. Perhaps you recognize yourself in the freefall of worry that Danusha Laméris conveys in "Thinking" (47). Wherever you find yourself barring your own path to inner peace, ask yourself with Rumi, "Why do you stay in prison/when the door is so wide open?" (27).

Write a poem about a time when you noticed you were standing in your own way, and how you freed yourself.

POEMS FOR INSPIRATION:

- "A Community of the Spirit," Rumi (translation by Coleman Barks), 27.
- "Thinking," Danusha Laméris, 47.

- "Because even the word *obstacle* is an obstacle," Alison Luterman, 88.
- "Mind Wanting More," Holly J. Hughes, 89.
- "Moth Koan," Richard Schiffman, 175.
- "At the Teahouse, 6 am," Holly J. Hughes, 176.

LAST POEM AND TESTAMENT

Write the poem you want to leave behind. What do you want your loved ones to know?

How will they find it? Neatly tucked away in a drawer? Attached to your Last Will and Testament? In the pocket of the coat you wore last winter?

The first time I offered this prompt in a workshop, participants were apprehensive. They found it challenging to imagine the scenario. But once they did, they found enormous gratification in expressing the essential thoughts they wanted their loved ones to know and remember. Without exception, each participant expressed the desire to tuck the poem away and make sure it would be found when the need arose.

This is not a prompt about death. It is a prompt about the lives you impact through your presence. Think of this poem as a timeless gift—a gift that few of us ever receive, and even fewer think to give.

* * *

Poems for inspiration:

- "Learning from Trees," Grace Butcher, 124.
- "Savasana: Corpse Pose," Marianne Murphy Zarzana, 125.
- "The Last Things I'll Remember," Joyce Sutphen, 172.

ON THE WINGS OF A SONG

Music engages our attention like few other experiences. It invites us into a physical relationship with sound. It changes the rhythm of our breath. We can't help swaying our body, moving our feet.

Think of how your body responds to a lullaby, a Gregorian chant, an aria, a folk song, a guitar solo at a rock concert.

When has music touched you in a profound way? Write a poem that translates your experience of music into words. While you will certainly want to rely on the sense of sound, remember to include the other senses as well. Do you get goosebumps when a tenor hits a high note? Does a folk song conjure up visual images? Does a particular song trigger a memory? Use specific details to create memorable images. Let your poem sing, and inspire your reader to sing along!

POEMS FOR INSPIRATION:

- "The Second Music," Annie Lighthart, 36.
- "Untitled (This is what was bequeathed us)," Gregory Orr, 37.

- "Versions of Ghalib: Ghazal I," Ghalib (translation by Ruth L. Schwartz), 85.
- "My Father at the Piano," Mary O'Connor, 159.
- "Parallel the Care the Dancer Takes," Hafiz (translation by Daniel Ladinksy), 160.

28

'TIS THE SEASON

Poems about specific seasons can help anchor us to concrete images and memories. What makes spring different from fall? Winter from spring? What are the smells associated with each season? What emotions are triggered by these words: Leaves? Snow? Forsythia? Beach?

Read the following selections from *Poetry of Presence* and notice the details used to depict each season. How does your experience of a season differ?

Write a poem about one of the seasons. Engage as many senses as possible. Try using one of them in an unexpected way. What does winter taste like? What is the sound of a summer day?

POEMS FOR INSPIRATION:

Winter

- "Winter Poem," Nikki Giovanni, 94.
- "On the Necessity of Snow Angels for the Well-Being of the World," Grace Butcher, 106.

- "Winter Grace," Patricia Fargnoli, 157.

Spring

- "Camas Lilies," Lynn Ungar, 95.
- "St. Francis and the Sow," Galway Kinnell, 96.
- "Flowering," Linda Buckmaster, 133.

Summer

- "Minobimaadizi," Kimberly Blaeser, 121.
- "Rain on Water," Freya Manfred, 127.
- "Soundings," Joyce Sutphen, 138.

Fall

- "Praise Song," Barbara Crooker, 45.
- "Midlife," Julie Cadwallader Staub, 83.
- "What Else," Carolyn Locke, 183.

WHAT IS MORE GENEROUS THAN A WINDOW?

Pat Schneider concludes "The Patience of Ordinary Things" with a very evocative question: "What is more generous than a window?" (33). Ponder that question as you consider some of the sights you have witnessed through a window.

Write a poem about the view from your favorite window. What do you see when you look though it? Look out the same window at different times of day. How does the view change? What mood does it call up? What do you hope to see when you look out?

POEMS FOR INSPIRATION:

- "The Patience of Ordinary Things," Patricia Schneider, 33.
- "Twilight," Louise Glück, 143.
- "Putting in a Window," John Brantingham, 169.
- "At the Teahouse, 6 am," Holly J. Hughes, 176.

(Used in Week 7 Workshop, page 152 in this guide)

.

THE LAST SHALL BE FIRST

A great poem will leave you wanting more. More encounters with the world the poet has created. More time in her or his company. More conversation with the human, animal, or botanical beings that populate the poem.

For this exercise, choose the last line of a poem in *Poetry of Presence*, and make it the first line of a poem of your own. Where might that poem lead you? How can you continue the conversation? The following examples all offer evocative closing lines that could serve as an exciting starting point for a new poem.

POEMS FOR INSPIRATION:

- "The Patience of Ordinary Things," Pat Schneider, 33.
- "The Thing Is," Ellen Bass, 154.
- "Walking a Field into Evening," Larry Smith, 164.
- "There was a time I would reject those," Muhyiddin Ibn Al-'Arabi (translator unknown), 193.

31

LEARNING TO LISTEN

Listening is vitally important to the practice of mindfulness. Often in the noise of modern life, we are so busy trying to hear that we forget to listen. We forget to focus on what Annie Lighthart calls "The Second Music," which is "perhaps more faithful for being less heard/yet always present" (36).

As you reflect on the following selections from *Poetry of Presence*, listen to your surroundings. What do you hear? The wind chimes in the backyard? The hum of the fan on the windowsill? The water coming to a boil in the kettle? Take some time to rest in the sounds that surround you. Then try to capture those sounds in a poem. Are they music or noise? Do they enhance or distract?

POEMS FOR INSPIRATION:

- "The Second Music," Annie Lighthart, 36.
- "Rankin Ridge," Linda M. Hasselstrom, 136.
- "Listening Deeply," Dick Allen, 137.
- "Soundings," Joyce Sutphen, 138.
- "Walking a Field into Evening," Larry Smith, 164.

32

BELOVED COMMUNITY

Dr. Martin Luther King, Jr. spoke of the need to create a beloved community. This goal resonates through many of the works in *Poetry of Presence*. From Rumi to Ríos, poets have offered visions of that beloved community and our role in creating it.

Read the following selections and write a poem about your vision of a beloved community. What does the phrase mean to you? Who does it include? What does it mean to be in community with other species? How might a sense of community change the world? How might mindfulness help bring about these changes?

POEMS FOR INSPIRATION:

- "A Community of the Spirit," Rumi (translation by Coleman Barks), 27.
- "We Are of a Tribe," Alberto Ríos, 51.
- "Lakol Wicoun," Lydia Whirlwind Soldier, 72.
- "Think of Others," Mahmoud Darwish (translation by Mohammad Shaheen), 142.
- "For the Sake of Strangers," Dorianne Laux, 153.

33

EVERYDAY MIRACLES

What is a miracle? How do you define it? In "Miracle Fair" Wislawa Szymborska tells us it is a miracle "that so many commonplace miracles happen" (98). What miracles will you notice today?

Read the following selections from *Poetry of Presence*. Write a list-poem of miracles that you might have missed as you were driving to the supermarket or doing the laundry. Let yourself be surprised and delighted. Choose one item on the list and develop it into another poem.

Try writing a poem about a different item on the list each day for a week. What do you notice? It might just be miraculous!

POEMS FOR INSPIRATION:

- "A Little Stone in the Middle of the Road, in Florida," Muriel Rukeyser, 38.
- "Praise Song," Barbara Crooker, 45.
- "Camas Lilies," Lynn Ungar, 95.
- "Miracle Fair," Wislawa Szymborska (translation by Joanna Trzeciak), 98.

- "Feather at Midday," Sister Dang Nghiem, 100.
- "The Good News," Thich Nhat Hanh, 151.

(Used in Week 3 Workshop, page 147 of this guide)

WHAT THE GEESE KNOW

There is something elemental about geese. They are pervasive in American poetry, from our earliest adventures with Mother Goose to the "Hope ... borne on wings" in Barbara Crooker's "Sometimes, I Am Startled Out of Myself" (165).

What is it that makes us stop and listen when we hear them passing overhead in that geometrical V-formation? Is it their speed and grace? Or the way they coordinate their flight, sharing the burden of leadership, knowing when to yield, when to advance? Why shouldn't we pay attention? Wasn't it a goose that laid the golden egg?

Read the five poems listed below and recall a moment when you looked up in wonder at the sound or sight of geese overhead. What was it that made you stop what you were doing and allow yourself to be fully present in that moment? Write a poem about it.

POEMS FOR INSPIRATION:

- "Bali Hai Calls Mama," Marilyn Nelson, 34.

- "Listening Deeply," Dick Allen, 137.
- "Walking a Field into Evening," Larry Smith, 164.
- "Sometimes, I Am Startled Out of Myself," Barbara Crooker, 165.
- "Fog," Twyla M. Hansen, 179.

THE MUSIC OF BREATH

Hannah Stephenson tells us, "breathing is/the most ancient language" (29). There is no sound more universal than the breath. It is our first music; it is our final note.

We think of breathing as something that occurs automatically, and, of course, it does. But conscious breathing can be practiced as an intentional form of mindfulness meditation.

Spend some time today in mindful awareness of your breath. Experiment with the pace and rhythm. Hold your breath for a count of three between inhalation and exhalation. Feel the changes conscious breathing creates in your body and your state of mind. Write about the things you notice. Translate a poem from that "ancient language."

POEMS FOR INSPIRATION:

- "Ancient Language," Hannah Stephenson, 29.
- "The Cure for It All," Julia Fehrenbacher, 40.
- "Wage Peace," Judyth Hill, 182.

3 6

TO LOVE THE EARTH

From intimacy to awe, poems that evoke the love of the Earth resonate with reverence and mindfulness. Nancy Paddock invites us to "Lie down with your belly to the ground" (32). Seamus Heaney reminds us that when we fully engage with the majesty of nature, it will inevitably "catch the heart off guard and blow it open" (101).

Read the following selections and write a poem in the form of a letter to the Earth. Address the letter "Dear Mother," and express your awe, gratitude, and commitment to her care.

Then write a second poem-letter, this one from the Earth to you. Begin with the words "Dear Child." Listen to what the Earth wants you to know.

POEMS FOR INSPIRATION:

- "Lie Down," Nancy Paddock, 32.
- "Untitled (This is what was bequeathed us)," Gregory Orr, 37.
- "Testimony," Rebecca Baggett, 67.
- "Lakol Wicoun," Lydia Whirlwind Soldier, 72.

- "Visiting Mountains," Ted Kooser, 73.
- "Postscript," Seamus Heaney, 101.
- "Another Ocean," Ruby R. Wilson, 161.
- "When I Am Wise," Mary Gray, 173.
- "An Observation," May Sarton, 181.

OVERCOMING ANXIETY

Political unrest, racial injustice, a worldwide pandemic, economic instability ... is it any wonder that so many of us are struggling with anxiety in these turbulent times?

Several selections in *Poetry of Presence* explore the sources of anxiety in our modern world and offer insights to help us cope. Can you find yourself in any of these poems? What does anxiety feel like to you?

Spend some time in quiet contemplation. Take a few deep breaths and try to bring yourself into a state of calm. How does this feeling differ from anxiety?

Write a poem focusing on how mindfulness can help ease the pain of anxiety. Use specific images to convey the stress and the struggle to overcome it. Make the poem a roadmap to help you find your way back to peace when you are in worry's grip.

Poems for inspiration:

- "Thinking," Danusha Laméris, 47.

- "Because even the word *obstacle* is an obstacle," Alison Luterman, 88.
- "Trough," Judy Sorum Brown, 128.
- "Moth Koan," Richard Schiffmann, 175.
- "Wage Peace," Judyth Hill, 182.
- "For Calling the Spirit Back from Wandering the Earth in Its Human Feet," Joy Harjo, 189.

(Used in Week 9 Workshop, page 154 of this guide)

3 8

ROUTINE RITUALS

What is the difference between a routine and a ritual?

For years, I woke up when the alarm went off, fixed myself a cup of coffee, listened to the news, and sat on the couch until I had enough energy to start my day. It was my routine until I noticed that whenever I woke up before dawn, there was something peaceful and centering about that time. I sipped my coffee slowly, sitting cross-legged in the corner of the sofa, looking out at the trees beyond our backyard.

As my body developed a new rhythm, I began waking up at 5:00 a.m. most days without the aid of an alarm clock. Little by little, I had developed a ritual. Now there is something sacred about that time. If I wake up late (meaning after the sun is up), I feel a sense of loss. Even though my actions aren't all that different, the intention has changed. Rising early and starting my day with contemplative time has become a spiritual practice.

Read the following selections from *Poetry of Presence* and consider the rituals you discover in them. Some are mysterious; some are mundane. All invite us to pay attention and fully appreciate our actions and surroundings in the context of something larger than ourselves. They invite us to recognize the power of practice.

Think of a routine in which you engage on a regular basis. How can you infuse it with the qualities of ritual? Write a poem in which you create a ritual out of a simple daily activity.

POEMS FOR INSPIRATION:

- "Lie Down," Nancy Paddock, 32.
- "On the Necessity of Snow Angels for the Well-Being of the World," Grace Butcher, 106.
- "I Am Going to Start Living Like a Mystic," Edward Hirsch, 108.
- "The Uncertainty Principle," Kathleen Norris, 109.
- "Minobimaadizi," Kimberly Blaeser, 121.
- "Wakarusa Medicine Wheel," Denise Low, 135.
- "Parallel the Care the Dancer Takes," Hafiz (translation by Daniel Ladinsky), 160.

HONORING THE SACRED

Nearly 700 years ago, the Persian poet Hafiz wrote:

Now is the time for the world to know
That every thought and action is sacred. (110)

This sentiment is echoed in numerous selections from *Poetry of Presence*. Whether it is Tom Barrett declaring that "the sacred can't be contained" (70), or Wendell Berry observing that "There are no unsacred places" (103), these poems challenge us to find the sacred in all things and all creatures.

Where do you encounter the sacred? Is it in a church, temple, or mosque? Is it in a rowboat on a lake at sunset? Is it in the eyes of your loved ones? Spend some time contemplating the sacred spaces in your life. Write a poem about one of them. Notice the qualities that make it sacred to you. Be as specific as possible. For an additional challenge, create the sense of the sacred without using the word.

* * *

POEMS FOR INSPIRATION:

- "A Sacrament," Paulann Petersen, 56.
- "What's in the Temple?," Tom Barrett, 70.
- "Lakol Wicoun," Lydia Whirlwind Soldier, 72.
- "Still," A. R. Ammons, 79.
- "How to Be a Poet," Wendell Berry, 103.
- "The Uncertainty Principle," Kathleen Norris, 109.
- "Now is the Time," Hafiz (translation by Daniel Ladinsky), 110.

A BEND IN THE RIVER

An African proverb says, "You can't step into the same river twice." One reason is that the river is constantly changing through its own motion; another reason is that we are always changing, and we ourselves are different each time we step into the current.

Maybe that's why poets have always been fascinated by rivers. They follow a path that mirrors our lives. They are full of unexpected twists and turns, or what John O'Donohue calls "the surprise/ Of [their] own unfolding" (82).

Read the following selections from *Poetry of Presence* and imagine yourself floating down a river. Is it calm or turbulent? Are you paddling gently in a canoe, or roaring down the rapids in a raft? Where does it flow? What do you see on its banks? Write a poem to capture the feeling it evokes for you.

POEMS FOR INSPIRATION:

- "Afterwards," William Stafford, 64.
- "Fluent," John O'Donohue, 82.

- "Midlife," Julie Cadwallader Staub, 83.
- "Journey," Linda Hogan, 194.

(Used in Week 6 Workshop, page 151 of this guide)

41

THE FAMILY CIRCLE

Whatever the lessons, our families are our first teachers. They are the mirrors in which we see ourselves, and sometimes they are the mirrors from which we must turn away to find out who we really are. Whatever else they are, families are complicated. Thus, poems about family work best when they reflect that complexity.

Writing about family is challenging because we want to tell the truth and avoid sentimentality and cliché.

The best poems about family are the ones that invite us into the relationships that have made us who we are. These poems rely on specific details and images. Instead of writing a poem that states "I love my mother," write a poem that helps the reader see and understand your love for your mother.

Poetry of Presence includes numerous poems that convey the beauty, depth, and complexity of family life. Read the following selections and contemplate the family relationships that are important to you. What do you want to say to, or about, a particular relative?

Look for an interesting way to begin the poem. For example, what happens when you sit next to a person on a plane who is wearing your sister's favorite perfume? What song on the radio takes you back to your father's workbench? What color conjures your mother's garden? When you walk down the hall in a hospital, do your footsteps remind you of the time you visited your grandmother in the ICU? Do the holidays fill you with joyful memories or painful ones? Why?

Be present with the memories. If it helps, spend some time thumbing through family photo albums. Capture the details, and when you are ready, write a poem that illuminates a relationship that is important to you.

POEMS FOR INSPIRATION:

- "Bali Hai Calls Mama," Marilyn Nelson, 34.
- "Prayer for the Dead," Stuart Kestenbaum, 61.
- "Testimony," Rebecca Baggett, 67.
- "A Poem for My Daughter," Teddy Macker, 113.
- "My Father at the Piano," Mary O'Connor, 159.
- "Saying Our Names," Marianne Murphy Zarzana, 163.
- "Mimesis," Fady Joudah, 192.

42

WHAT THE INSECTS CAN TEACH US

I'll just come out and say it: bugs have always freaked me out.

Then I met my now stepdaughter, Emily, who is an entomologist. This relationship has led me to rethink my viewpoint on bugs. A bee is no longer a flying weapon out to puncture tender flesh, but a highly specialized aviator, willing to lay down its life for the community. Ants are not picnic invaders but engineers, teaching us how to work together for the common good.

Reframing how I looked at insects gave me a surprising path into mindfulness. Understanding them requires patience, stillness, quiet, and an open mind. I don't know a better definition of presence.

Read the following selections from *Poetry of Presence* and contemplate the beauty and mystery of our insect neighbors. Allow yourself to be fascinated. They will not disappoint. Write an ode (an appreciation) to the insect, arachnid, or annelid of your choice.

POEMS FOR INSPIRATION:

- "A Sacrament," Paulann Petersen, 56.

- "Love for Other Things," Tom Hennen, 76.
- "The Mosquito Among the Raindrops," Teddy Macker, 92.
- "Earthworms," Lynn Ungar, 112.
- "Moth Koan," Richard Schiffman, 175.
- "Mimesis," Fady Joudah, 192.

43

AWAKENINGS

Mindfulness is about being fully awake. Every poem in *Poetry of Presence* has this theme at its core. But some poems focus on the precise moment of awakening, that moment when we are not just awake, but actually aware of our consciousness.

Can you recall a moment when you suddenly woke up, whether literally or metaphorically? What was the trigger? How did it change you? What happened when you suddenly knew you were awake?

Read the following selections from *Poetry of Presence*. Recall a moment when suddenly something (or everything) made sense. Write a poem that focuses on that moment. To paraphrase Barbara Crooker, find a way to be startled out of yourself.

POEMS FOR INSPIRATION:

- "The Way It Is," Lynn Ungar, 31.
- "Meditation on a Grapefruit," Craig Arnold, 39.
- "Getting Up Early," Anne Porter, 66.
- "*Ich liebe meines Wesens Dunkelstunden* (I love the dark hours

of my being)," Rainer Maria Rilke (translation by Anita Barrows and Joanna Macy), 131.

- "Meeting the Light Completely," Jane Hirshfield, 140.
- "Sometimes, I Am Startled Out of Myself," Barbara Crooker, 165.
- "No More Same Old Silly Love Songs," Neil Carpathios, 180.

44

ON RETEACHING A THING ITS LOVELINESS

In "St. Francis and the Sow," Galway Kinnell tells us, "sometimes it is necessary/to reteach a thing its loveliness" (96). As the poem delineates every tender feature of the nursing sow, Kinnell not only shows us the sow's beauty, he reminds us to turn that lens on many creatures whose beauty we might overlook—even ourselves.

Read the following selections from *Poetry of Presence* and think about what "loveliness" means to you. Write a poem celebrating the beauty of a creature whose loveliness we might otherwise forget to appreciate.

POEMS FOR INSPIRATION:

- "Love for Other Things," Tom Hennen, 76.
- "Still," A. R. Ammons, 79.
- "St. Francis and the Sow," Galway Kinnell, 96.
- "Earthworms," Lynn Ungar, 112.
- "The Thing Is," Ellen Bass, 154.
- "The Joins," Chana Bloch, 185.

EMBRACING BROKENNESS

In "I Will Keep Broken Things," Alice Walker writes:

> Their beauty
> is
> they
> need
> not
> ever
> be
> 'fixed.' (147)

Meditate on the broken things in your life. Do you keep them? Are they treasures or debris?

Think of some broken thing that you can't bear to discard. Spend some time contemplating it. Have you repaired it or left it broken? What does it feel like in your hands? What does it sound like when you pick it up and put it down? Do you handle it with reverence because of its brokenness?

Do the broken things in your life reflect some of your own brokenness? Where do you find yourself in need of repair? Are you trying to mend yourself? Or can you find the beauty in your brokenness?

Write a poem exploring something that is broken. How might the act of writing about it create a new kind of wholeness?

POEMS FOR INSPIRATION:

- "Plate," Al Zolynas, 145.
- "I Will Keep Broken Things," Alice Walker, 146.
- "The Way It Is," Rosemerry Wahtola Trommer, 149.
- "What Else," Carolyn Locke, 183.
- "The Joins," Chana Block, 185.

(Used in Week 2 Workshop, page 145 of this guide)

4 6

LOOKING TO THE SKIES

Poets have always looked to the skies for inspiration. What draws your attention there? Sunshine or moonlight? Patterns in the clouds? Do you look at airplanes and wonder where the passengers are going? Do they make you yearn for new destinations?

Spend some time today stargazing or just soaking up the sun. Write a poem that paints a picture of one of the sky's many moods. Think about the time of day or night, the colors, the way the light changes, the presence or absence of clouds. Focusing on a particular view of the sky will enable you to emphasize specific details and images that will make this moment of sky unlike any other.

POEMS FOR INSPIRATION:

- "We Are of a Tribe," Alberto Ríos, 51.
- "Getting Up Early," Anne Porter, 66.
- "Evening Star," Charles Goodrich, 97.
- "Feather at Midday," Sister Dang Nghiem, 100.
- "Consider the Space Between Stars," Linda Pastan, 156.
- "Moon," Billy Collins, 170.

THE GIFT OF UNCERTAINTY

True wisdom is rooted in the search for understanding rather than the assumption of truth. When we think we have all the answers, we stop seeking, stop learning. This kind of misguided certainty sets the stage for all kinds of havoc, as we see in the current climate of public discourse.

What is the benefit of not knowing? How might not knowing lead to wisdom? Write a poem about something you just cannot understand. Perhaps you will discover a new insight in the process. You just never know.

POEMS FOR INSPIRATION:

- "A Gift," Denise Levertov, 69.
- "The Uncertainty Principle," Kathleen Norris, 109.
- "The Place Where We are Right," Yehuda Amichai (translation by Chana Bloch and Stephen Mitchell), 111.
- "You Are There," Erica Jong, 123.
- "Putting in a Window," John Brantingham, 169.

IN THE PRESENCE OF LIGHT

Sunlight is a source of nourishment. It provides us with Vitamin D to support our blood and brain functions. Moonlight can guide us through the dark. No wonder light holds such strong appeal for poets who have tried to capture it in all its variations.

Light isn't just something we encounter outdoors. Consider how you feel in a room washed in candlelight as opposed to fluorescent lighting. Noticing the light is a way of being present.

Look out the nearest window right now. Is the light diffuse or direct? Do you need your sunglasses or a flashlight? How does the light make you feel? Embraced or exposed? Lost or found?

Spend ten minutes journaling about light. Then find a phrase in your journal entry that you would like to explore further. Turn it into a poem. Don't hide it under a bushel!

POEMS FOR INSPIRATION:

- "Praise Song," Barbara Crooker, 45.
- "Under Ideal Conditions," Al Zolynas, 60.
- "Still Life at Dusk," Rosemerry Wahtola Trommer, 65.

- "Twilight," Louise Glück, 143.
- "The Bright Field," R. S. Thomas, 150.
- "Solstice," Robyn Sarah, 158.
- "Saying Our Names," Marianne Murphy Zarzana, 163.
- "Moon," Billy Collins, 170.
- "Moth Koan," Richard Schiffman, 175.

EMBODIED PRESENCE

In Western culture we tend to think of the body and the mind as separate entities. Mindfulness urges us to recognize that the two are inextricably linked. Many of the works in *Poetry of Presence* invite us to consider the miraculous capabilities of the human body. These poems are rooted in day-to-day physical activities: walking, swimming, breathing, eating, stretching.

Mindfulness invites us to be fully present in the body with all its strength, weakness, beauty, and variations, while also recognizing its vulnerability to illness and the graceful passage into death.

Spend a day actively observing the things your body does for you. How it stands, sits, walks, lifts a baby, bends to pet a dog. Choose one physical action that you do every day but seldom think about. Write a poem celebrating that action. Describe it in vivid detail. Imagine that you are a choreographer, and the poem is your dance. Feel every muscle as it comes to life in this single action.

* * *

POEMS FOR INSPIRATION:

- "Lie Down," Nancy Paddock, 32.
- "Visiting Mountains," Ted Kooser, 73.
- "Stone," Danusha Laméris, 91.
- "On the Necessity of Snow Angels for the Well-Being of the World," Grace Butcher, 106.
- "When I Taught Her How to Tie Her Shoes," Penny Harter, 107.
- "Savasana: Corpse Pose," Marianne Murphy Zarzana, 125.
- "Rain on Water," Freya Manfred, 127.
- "No Fishing," David Allan Evans, 167.
- "An Observation," May Sarton, 181.
- "Bedside Manners," Christopher Wiseman, 187.

WHERE POETRY RESIDES

Where did *that* come from? It's a question many of us have asked after reading or writing a poem that seems to have come in a flash of divine inspiration. These are the poems that make us believe that the Muse must have had a hand in it. But poetic inspiration doesn't reside on Mt. Olympus. It resides in our own mindful musings.

Wendell Berry tells us that poetry begins when we "Breathe with unconditional breath" (103). Rilke tells us to "step out of doors … Out of the room that lets you feel secure" (162).

Where do you find inspiration? Do you have a favorite time or place where you write? Do you find your inspiration in nature? Music? Paintings? Do you have a writing practice or do you wait for a spark to ignite your imagination?

Write a poem about what inspires you to write poetry. Keep it close at hand for times when you need a little reminder that poetry is always there for you, whether you're reading, writing, or offering it to others.

* * *

POEMS FOR INSPIRATION:

- "On How to Pick and Eat Poems," Phyllis Cole-Dai, 21.
- "What's in the Temple?," Tom Barrett, 70.
- "The Muse Is a Little Girl," Marjorie Saiser, 102.
- "How to Be a Poet," Wendell Berry, 103.
- "Parallel the Care the Dancer Takes," Hafiz (translated by Daniel Ladinsky), 160.
- "Entrance," Rainer Maria Rilke (translation by Dana Gioia), 162.

PART III: FOR WORKSHOP FACILITATORS

This section is for workshop facilitators. It lays out both general guidelines and specific lesson plans for a 12-week *Poetry of Presence* immersion course that places the poems in conversation with each other as well as with members of the group. It includes much journaling, but it focuses on experiential reading and contemplation. Writing is a tool rather than a goal.

Think of this outline as a roadmap. You always have the option of choosing alternate routes.

The workshop is a response to the critical issues that have arisen in the wake of the Covid-19 pandemic and the feelings of anxiety and helplessness it has brought for so many. It is a response to fear, suffering, loss and grief. It seeks to create a balance between those very pressing issues and the reality that there is still so much reason for hope and many pathways to inner peace.

As Rebecca Baggett says in "Testimony," "the world is still beautiful" (67), even in the face of suffering and devastation. Addressing her daughters, that poem goes on to say, "I want/you to understand that you are/no more and no less necessary/than the brown recluse, the ruby-/throated hummingbird, the humpback/whale, the profligate mimosa" (67). Baggett wants her daughters to know that they are part of that beautiful world, as she concludes with the lines:

> ...I still believe
> we are capable of attention,
> that anyone who notices the world
> must want to save it. (68)

Mindfulness begins with noticing. Such is the invitation inherent in every poem in *Poetry of Presence,* and it is the invitation inherent in this workshop. Notice the world. Notice it with all your senses. Let it thrill and surprise you.

Above all, this is a listening workshop.

We listen to the poems.
We listen to the poets.
We listen to each other.
We listen to our hearts.

We want to be part of a conversation with the poems that move us. And guess what? Most people who take the workshop just can't help but write their own poems as well. Whether the goal is publication, personal sharing, or private reflection, the desire for self-expression is contagious.

INTRODUCTION

This section is for workshop facilitators. It lays out both general guidelines and specific lesson plans for a 12-week *Poetry of Presence* immersion course that places the poems in conversation with each other as well as with members of the group. It includes much journaling, but it focuses on experiential reading and contemplation. Writing is a tool rather than a goal.

Think of this outline as a roadmap. You always have the option of choosing alternate routes.

The workshop is a response to the critical issues that have arisen in the wake of the Covid-19 pandemic and the feelings of anxiety and helplessness it has brought for so many. It is a response to fear, suffering, loss and grief. It seeks to create a balance between those very pressing issues and the reality that there is still so much reason for hope and many pathways to inner peace.

As Rebecca Baggett says in "Testimony," "the world is still beautiful" (67), even in the face of suffering and devastation. Addressing her daughters, that poem goes on to say, "I want/you to understand that you are/no more and no less necessary/than the brown recluse, the ruby-/throated hummingbird, the humpback/whale, the profligate mimosa" (67). Baggett wants her daughters to know that they are part of that beautiful world, as she concludes with the lines:

> ...I still believe
> we are capable of attention,
> that anyone who notices the world
> must want to save it. (68)

Mindfulness begins with noticing. Such is the invitation inherent in every poem in *Poetry of Presence,* and it is the invitation inherent in this workshop. Notice the world. Notice it with all your senses. Let it thrill and surprise you.

Above all, this is a listening workshop.

> *We listen to the poems.*
> *We listen to the poets.*
> *We listen to each other.*
> *We listen to our hearts.*

We want to be part of a conversation with the poems that move us. And guess what? Most people who take the workshop just can't help but write their own poems as well. Whether the goal is publication, personal sharing, or private reflection, the desire for self-expression is contagious.

CORE PRINCIPLES

It is helpful to establish these core principles during the first session:

1. Show up.

2. Experience the poems.

3. There are no assignments, only invitations.

4. We are not here to fix anyone; just share and listen.

5. Do only what feels safe and comfortable.

WORKSHOP SUPPLIES AND LOGISTICS

SUPPLIES

It is helpful if each participant has a copy of *Poetry of Presence*, a journal or notebook, and a pen or pencil (or writing device). As facilitator, you will need a timer. I also use a brass singing bowl to begin and end each segment of silence and writing.

SESSION STRUCTURE

This guide is based on 90-minute workshop sessions. This time frame works well with a group of 5-10 participants. It can be expanded to accommodate a larger group. A workshop session focuses on three poems to explore a particular theme or topic. The first poem is an introduction to the theme. The second poem serves as the basis for the *Lectio Poetica* process (described below). The third poem serves as the closing. A typical 90-minute session includes the following:

   Silent centering (5 min.)
   Introduction of the theme (5 min.)

Reading of opening poem (5 min.)
Introduction of *Lectio Poetica* process (5 min.)
Lectio Poetica process (60 min.), including:

> Three readings of *Lectio* poem (15 min.)
> Silent reflection on poem (5 min.)
> Written reflection (20 min.)
> Sharing reflections (20 min.)

Closing poem (5 min.)
Silent centering (5 min.)

The lesson plans provide themes and selections that I have used following this format. The prompts and subject index are useful in developing additional sessions, if you choose.

Silent Centering (5 minutes)

The workshop begins with silent centering. I am careful not to use the word meditation because many people are intimidated by it. They can get caught up in "doing it right," which becomes an obstacle. I prefer to describe this period as a threshold into a quiet space. This phase is particularly helpful in an online workshop environment, where it takes some time to switch gears and become fully present. If you are using an online platform such as Zoom, remember to ask participants to mute themselves during silent centering and writing periods to minimize distractions.

Introduction of the Theme and Reading of the Opening Poem (10 minutes)

Introduce the theme and announce the titles of the poems that will be used during the session. This step helps set the tone for the readings and reflections by establishing a context. Then read the opening poem aloud, inviting the group to just listen. They don't need to follow along in the book. After the first reading, there is a brief pause, and then a member of the group reads it a second time.

This time, participants are asked to read along in the book. Participants are invited to comment briefly if they choose.

Introduction of the Lectio Poetica Process (5 minutes)

The centerpiece of each session is *Lectio Poetica,* an adaptation of the ancient contemplative practice of *Lectio Divina.* In developing this workshop, I have drawn on the work of Jay and Barbara Valusek, whose model is available at http://lectio.jayevalusek.com/about-us.html. Their format reflects the Christian tradition from which it is derived. In adapting their work, I have created an abridged version that is appropriate for both religious and non-religious participants.

The Lectio Poetica Process (60 minutes)

Much of the power of the *Lectio* practice comes from the repetition of the selected poem, which is read aloud three times by different readers. As the facilitator, you read it first. Before you begin reading, ask for volunteers for the second and third readings so the process flows smoothly.

Repetition of the poem helps the listener connect with it in a variety of ways. Hearing the poem read in multiple voices with a variety of inflections and rhythms creates different points of interest each time. Participants often notice new words and phrases with each reading.

During the first reading, ask participants to simply listen and focus on the words of the poem. After a quiet pause of 60 seconds or so, the second person reads the poem while the group follows along in the book. After another pause, the third person reads the poem while participants are asked to notice what words or phrases stand out to them. In the terminology of the *Lectio Poetica* practice, ask the participants to contemplate "the words or phrases that shimmer."

After completing the third reading, invite the participants to spend 3-5 minutes silently contemplating the poem with particular emphasis on those words and phrases they noted. It is important to be flexible on the timing because some group members are eager to jump right into the writing process. Others prefer to ponder and reflect before they pick up the pen. In either case, it is important to have a contemplative pause before the writing begins.

After the pause, invite those who are ready to begin writing. Ask them to consider the "shimmer" words as a starting point. Remind them that a prompt is never an assignment. This writing is whatever they need or want it to be. In addition, they should never feel like they are being asked to produce a poem. I have seen people create amazing poems in response to a *Lectio* reading, and it is always welcome. But it is important to stress that this is not an expectation. No demands. No pressure.

The 20-minute writing period can be expanded if participants need more time. The pacing should be gentle and flexible.

Following the writing period, invite participants to share their work. Some may offer a summary of their reflections; some will read verbatim from their journal entry. Some may choose not to speak. This is their time.

Your most important role is to create a safe space and to ensure that everyone who chooses to participate is able to do so without judgment and without advice. The workshop is not, nor should it ever be, group therapy. Neither you nor the participants are in the workshop to fix anyone.

The Closing Poem and Silent Centering (10 minutes)

After everyone who chooses to has spoken, read the closing poem. Follow this reading with another five minutes of silent centering, during which the participants re-read the poem silently. Once again, ask them to identify a word or phrase that "shimmers" for them. After a minute or so, invite each member to say the word or phrase that struck them. There is no discussion; participants simply say the word or phrase. Often there will be repetition. Let them know that repetition is perfectly okay.

Invite the group to notice the rhythm that develops in this single word/phrase sharing. These small closing phrases provide a synthesis of what each participant has experienced during the workshop session. The effect of this series of words is similar to the utterance of "Amen" at the end of a prayer. It signals closure.

BETWEEN SESSIONS

While there is no formal homework for this workshop, encourage participants to read a poem a day from the anthology and journal about it for 5-10 minutes. Invite them to notice particular lines that move them. Encourage them to keep a list of those lines for the culminating project: a cento composed of lines from *Poetry of Presence*. (The cento is explained below.)

This daily practice should never feel burdensome. Remind them that it is an invitation and not an assignment. Encourage them to view this reading time as a gift of presence, a gift that no one else can give them.

THE CULMINATING PROJECT:
WRITING A CENTO

A cento is a poem composed of lines from other poems. The name comes from the Latin word for "patchwork." As a culminating project, I think of the cento as a patchwork quilt that provides comfort in challenging times. By stitching together the lines that are most important to him or her, each participant creates a finished piece that serves as a source of shelter and warmth.

As participants explore *Poetry of Presence*, they often find works that become their "go to" poems for centering, mindfulness, and peace of mind. Constructing a cento is a creative way to put those poems into conversation with each other, creating something new and personal.

In this workshop, all the lines in the cento must come from poems in *Poetry of Presence*. Encourage participants to choose at least half of their lines from poems that have not been discussed in a workshop session. This goal encourages them to focus on a wider variety of source poems and makes for a diverse exchange when they present their centos during the final session.

JOYS AND CHALLENGES

Writing a cento is like directing a choir in which each singer has a solo line to sing, yet somehow what emerges is one beautifully cohesive song. In a cento, each individual line comes from a different poem.

Invite workshop participants to aim for a cento of 24-30 lines chosen from the 150 poems in *Poetry of Presence*. If each of the anthologized poems averages 20 lines (and that is a very rough estimate), we are looking at a minimum of 3,000 lines from which to choose. While I am not much of a math whiz, even I know that this equation asks the participant to choose less than 10% of the lines in the book. It can feel like a very daunting task.

This prompt reminds me of pictures I have seen of Dutch tulip farms in springtime. Just imagine it: thousands of flowers, stunning colors in glorious shapes and sizes. Then someone says, "Okay, choose ten percent of these blossoms and arrange them in a vase." Yikes! Where to begin? But that challenge is also the beauty of the cento. In this poetic form, the *process* is every bit as important and satisfying as the product. Tell the group to imagine they are strolling through those magnificent flowers. Remind them that it takes time. They need to go slowly as they contemplate each blossom. They want to look inside the cups of the tulips. See how the light penetrates the petals. By the time they make their choices, they have enjoyed a rewarding process of contemplation and discovery.

ELEMENTS OF A CENTO

THE TITLE

The title of the cento can either be a line from a poem, or an invented title that conveys the theme of the poem.

THE POEM

In this case, the poem consists of 24-30 individual lines chosen from the 150 poems in *Poetry of Presence*.

THE GLOSS

Because the cento is composed of other people's work, it is important to cite the source material. Explain to the group that each line of the cento must be credited to the original author in a gloss at the end of the poem. There are several reasons for this step. On a purely practical level, we always acknowledge the artist when excerpting their work; that practice is both a courtesy and a rule. Otherwise, if we publish our cento, we're engaging in plagiarism and/or copyright infringement. But even if we don't plan to publish, the cento's gloss is important. It's our way of thanking the source of inspiration. It is not just a list of footnotes; it is a compilation of gratitude. The gloss is also a roadmap back to a special place. After all, if we love a line enough to put it into the cento, we probably love it enough to want to revisit the poem from which it comes.

At the end of the cento, the full citation for the book should be provided as the first line of the gloss:

> Cole-Dai, Phyllis, and Ruby R. Wilson, eds. *Poetry of Presence: An Anthology of Mindfulness Poems.* Grayson Books, 2017. Print.

Each line is then attributed to its source poem within the anthology. The gloss includes the line number in the cento, the title of the source poem in quotations marks, the author's name, and the page number in *Poetry of Presence.* For example:

> Line 1 "The Patience of Ordinary Things," Pat Schneider, 33.

Since all the lines come from poems in the anthology, it is not necessary to repeat the book title for each citation.

SAMPLE CENTOS

INTRODUCTION TO THE CENTOS

The following centos were created by members of recent workshops. The participants in these workshops arrived at the process from various levels of writing experience. Some are accomplished poets; some are avid readers who had never written a poem before; some are completely new to both reading and writing poetry.

Without exception, participants found the exercise gratifying. They explained that the process of searching for and compiling lines that had strong personal meaning for them created a more rewarding encounter with each poem.

I recommend this exercise as a culminating project because it enables all participants, regardless of their writing experience, to create a tangible product that has both personal and artistic merit. With the cento, participants don't have to start from square one. This process can serve as a springboard into writing their own poems.

The process of bringing multiple voices together in a unified message of mindfulness and peace is an inspiring metaphor of hope for our fractured and fractious world. It shows us what is possible when we take the time to listen for the messages that unite us.

And one more thing: writing a cento is a whole lot of fun!

"PRECIOUS BREATH"

MEI TOW LAM

(a cento composed from poems in *Poetry of Presence)*

Breathing is the most ancient language.
Sit, close your eyes, breathe; go gently today, don't hurry.
Thinking nothing, transparent air.
The forest breathes, listen.
It knows everything.
Whatever it is the trees know when they stand undone.
These mountains listen,
an audience of thousands holding its breath in each rock.
We sit together, the mountain and me.
Take a breath offered by friendly winds ... give it back with
gratitude.
Gently, I blew a soft breath.
Breathe with unconditional breath.
Time does not move, the sky is not blue-
the end of the spectrum and beginning of light—
it is all in us, breathed in, let go.
The air moves back from you like a wave and you can't breathe.
Breathe in the damp musty air,

even when you were breathing hard, you were at rest.
Joy even in just this breathing.
Pay attention only to breath—
let it become a ribbon, the texture of fine silk.
For once on the face of the earth, let's not speak in any language.
The good news is that you are alive!
Look up, stay awhile; let your breathing slow.
Breathe in, breathe out.
Breathe until you stop needing anything to be different.

GLOSS: "PRECIOUS BREATH"

Cole-Dai, Phyllis, and Ruby R. Wilson, eds. *Poetry of Presence: An Anthology of Mindfulness Poems.* Grayson Books, 2017. Print.

1 "Ancient Language," Hannah Stephenson, 29.
2 "The Cure for It All," Julia Fehrenbacher, 40.
3 "Lessons from Darkness," Anita Barrows, 46.
4 "Lost," David Wagoner, 49.
5 "Journey," Linda Hogan, 194.
6 "Learning from Trees," Grace Butcher, 124.
7 "Visiting Mountains," Ted Kooser, 73.
8 "Visiting Mountains," Ted Kooser, 73.
9 "Zazen on Ching-t'ing Mountain," Li Po (translation by Sam Hamill), 122.
10 "For Calling the Spirit Back from Wandering the Earth in Its Human Feet," Joy Harjo, 189.
11 "Feather at Midday," Sister Dang Nghiem, 100.
12 "How to Be a Poet," Wendell Berry, 103.
13 "The Uncertainty Principle," Kathleen Norris, 109.
14 "The Uncertainty Principle," Kathleen Norris, 109.
15 "The Uncertainty Principle," Kathleen Norris, 109.
16 "The Moment," Margaret Atwood, 134.
17 "Walking a Field into Evening," Larry Smith, 164.

18 "You Are There," Erica Jong, 123.

19 "One's Ship Comes In," Joe Paddock, 129.

20 "Savasana: Corpse Pose," Marianne Murphy Zarzana, p. 125.

21 "Savasana: Corpse Pose," Marianne Murphy Zarzana, p. 125.

22 "Keeping quiet," Pablo Neruda, 104.

23 "The Good News," Thich Nhat Hanh, 151.

24 "We Are of a Tribe," Alberto Ríos, 51.

25 "The Cure for It All," Julia Fehrenbacher, 40.

26 "The Cure for It All," Julia Fehrenbacher, 40.

"ADVICE I WISH I HAD RECEIVED FORTY YEARS AGO"

JUDY CARR

(An Abecedarian* Cento Composed of Lines from *Poetry of Presence)*

Among your duties, pleasure is a thing
Beloved on the earth.
Cut the ties you have to failure and shame.
Don't you wish they would stop, all the thoughts,
Even the way that I believe the day.
Find the lowly nearby,
God comes to you disguised as your life.
Here in the heart
It's all so simple really,
Joy it will be.
Keep walking.
Look up, stay awhile. Let your breathing slow.
Must ask permission to know it and be known
No matter what you do, no matter what happens
One morning you might wake up.
Perhaps the earth can teach us.
Quit acting like a wolf and feel and
Return to teach me the meaning of life

Stay away from screens.
That and the beloved's clear instructions
Understand about what's happening,
Vanishing years, filled with light.
Wisdom is seeing the shape of your life
[Xactly] what it is,
Yet always present
Zigzagging, no ducking, no hiding under eaves.

* *An abecedarian is a poem in which the first letter of each line is arranged in alphabetical order.*

Gloss: "Advice I Wish I Had Received Forty Years Ago"

Cole-Dai, Phyllis, and Ruby R. Wilson, eds. *Poetry of Presence: An Anthology of Mindfulness Poems.* Grayson Books, 2017. Print.

1 "The Word," Tony Hoagland, 41.
2 "Late Fragment," Raymond Carver, 120.
3 "For Calling the Spirit Back from Wandering the Earth in Its Human Feet," Joy Harjo, 189.
4 "Thinking," Danusha Laméris, 47.
5 "A Momentary Creed," W. S. Merwin, 87.
6 "Still," A. R. Ammons, 79.
7 "A Poem for My Daughter," Teddy Macker, 113.
8 "The Uncertainty Principle," Kathleen Norris, 109.
9 "Sunday Afternoon," Nancy Ann Schaefer, 43.
10 "One's Ship Comes In," Joe Paddock, 129.
11 "On the Necessity of Snow Angels for the Well-Being of the World," Grace Butcher, 106.
12 "We Are of a Tribe," Alberto Ríos, 51.
13 "Lost," David Wagoner, 49.
14 "A Poem for My Daughter," Teddy Macker, 113.
15 "The Way It Is," Lynn Ungar, 31.
16 "Keeping quiet," Pablo Neruda, 104.

17 "A Community of the Spirit," Rumi (translation by Coleman Barks), 27.
18 "When I Taught Her How to Tie Her Shoes," Penny Harter, 107.
19 "How to Be a Poet," Wendell Berry, 103.
20 "Untitled," Gregory Orr, 37.
21 "Bedside Manners," Christopher Wiseman, 187.
22 "Consider the Space Between Stars," Linda Pastan, 156.
23 "The Cure," Albert Huffstickler, 155.
24 "The Way It Is," Lynn Ungar, 31.
25 "The Second Music," Annie Lighthart, 36.
26 "The Mosquito Among the Raindrops," Teddy Macker, 92.

"PATHWAY THROUGH A TROUBLED WORLD"

ALICE IRWIN

(a cento composed from poems in *Poetry of Presence)*

We are here for a moment of a story that is longer than all of us,
A hurry through which known and strange things pass,
Each year harder to live within.
We are all struggling; none of us has gone far.
We pick our way over the skulls of small talk
Plunging into the mossy shallows.
We cannot see what guides us on our way
With eyes that have forgotten how to see.
Go slow. Watch out for thorns and bears.
It's easy to lose this tenderly unfolding moment.

Perhaps the earth can teach us.
The forest breathes. Listen. It answers.
The earth beneath us moves, quiet and wild
And all thoughts heal down to a low whistling.
Invisible birds sing to the memory of light.
The crisp voices of the orange and gold October leaves
      are laughing at death.

Put your ear to the wall of your heart;
Breathe until you stop needing anything to be different;
Sing healing songs for the earth that bleeds.
These songs are about forgetting dying and loss.

Blessings often arrive as trouble.
Get close to the things that slide away in the dark.
Try to love everything that gets in your way.
Though darkness gathers, praise our crazy fallen world,
That immensity waiting to receive whatever arrives with trust.
To live is to be uncertain.
There should be more time like this, to sit and dream.
All we do is pass through here, the best way we can.
Before death enters, hat in hand,
Turn me into song; sing me awake.

Gloss: "Pathway Through a Troubled World"

Cole-Dai, Phyllis, and Ruby R. Wilson, eds. *Poetry of Presence: An Anthology of Mindfulness Poems.* Grayson Books, 2017. Print.

1 "Prayer for the Dead," Stuart Kestenbaum, 61.
2 "Postscript," Seamus Heaney, 101.
3 "Meditation on a Grapefruit," Craig Arnold, 39.
4 "Untitled (The Guest is inside you)," Kabir, 52.
5 "Visiting Mountains," Ted Kooser, 73.
6 "One's Ship Comes In," Joe Paddock, 129.
7 "Longing," Julie Cadwallader Staub, 63.
8 "Entrance," Rainer Maria Rilke, 162.
9 "On How to Pick and Eat Poems," Phyllis Cole-Dai, 21.
10 "Instructions for the Journey," Pat Schneider, 144.
11 "Keeping quiet," Pablo Neruda, 105.
12 "Lost," David Wagoner, 49.
13 "We Are of a Tribe," Alberto Ríos, 51.

"LIFELONG LEARNING"

CLAUDIA CHANG

(a cento composed from poems in *Poetry of Presence*)

The good news is that your child is there before you,
You will love again the stranger who was your self,
    Open the screen door to free her.

God comes to you disguised as your life.
    Grab a bucket or basket and head for light,
    Lie down with your belly to the ground
    waiting patiently for my empty body to pass through.
    Move outside the tangle of fear-thinking
    Give up all the other worlds except the one
        to which you belong,
    watch your mind. Without training it might run away.

God is anything, even a little stone in the middle of the road.
    The forest breathes. Listen. It answers.
    Sparrows roost in a nearby jack oak. A night hawk calls,
    the feather gliding over the roof.
And that pit of unfilled longing in your heart

crumbles like burnt paper in your hands.

Maybe people have to go in and out of shadows,
    To wake when all is possible
      and they have time for gathering and holding
        the earth about their feet.
We plant seeds in the ground and dreams in the sky.

When Whitman wrote, "I sing the body electric,"
I want to stay in that music without striving or cover
    while from the moving silence of trees
      To call myself beloved, to feel myself.

Gloss: "Lifelong Learning"

Cole-Dai, Phyllis, and Ruby R. Wilson, eds. *Poetry of Presence: An Anthology of Mindfulness Poems.* Grayson Books, 2017. Print.

1 "The Good News," Thich Nhat Hanh, 151.
2 "Love After Love," Derek Walcott, 55.
3 "Sunday Afternoon," Nancy Ann Schaefer, 43.
4 "A Poem for My Daughter," Teddy Macker, 113.
5 "How to Pick and Eat Poems," Phyllis Cole-Dai, 21.
6 "Lie Down," Nancy Paddock, 32.
7 "For the Sake of Strangers," Dorianne Laux, 153.
8 "A Community of the Spirit," Rumi (translation by Coleman Barks), 27.
9 "Sweet Darkness," David Whyte, 152.
10 "For Calling the Spirit Back from Wandering the Earth in Its Human Feet," Joy Harjo, 189.
11 "A Little Stone in the Middle of the Road, in Florida," Muriel Rukeyser, 38.
12 "Lost," David Wagoner, 49.
13 "Wakarusa Medicine Wheel," Denise Low, 135.

"PRESENCE AND REVERENCE"

BOB SACKEL

(a cento composed from poems in *Poetry of Presence*)

Breathing is the most ancient language
Wage peace with your breath
For everything flowers, from within, of self-blessing!

To love life, to love it even when you have no stomach for it
To be filled with light, and to shine!
Praise the light.

The Universe is shot through in all parts by a single sort of love
The World was made to be free in
Don't try proving your love is bigger than the Grand Canyon.

Cut the ties you have to failure and shame.
Let the pain be pain.
Move outside the tangle of fear thinking. Live in silence.
Accept what comes from silence, make the best you can of it.
For once on the face of the earth, let's not speak in any language.
When the radio in my car broke I started to notice the trees.

When you find a good bush, bow to it, or take off your shoes.
That and the beloved's clear instructions:
　　　Turn me into song; sing me awake.
I want to stay in that music without striving or cover.

We sit together, the mountain and me,
Together we're letting go.
Not in our nature to know what is journey and what is arrival.
The self you leave behind is only a skin you have outgrown.
A prerequisite is: with all you touch, you touch as if it were sacred.
Feast on your life.

GLOSS: "PRESENCE AND REVERENCE"

Cole-Dai, Phyllis, and Ruby R. Wilson, eds. *Poetry of Presence: An Anthology of Mindfulness Poems.* Grayson Books, 2017. Print.

1 "Ancient Language," Hannah Stephenson, 29.
2 "Wage Peace," Judyth Hill, 182.
3 "Saint Francis and the Sow," Galway Kinnell, 96.
4 "The Thing Is," Ellen Bass, 154.
5 "When I Am Among the Trees," Mary Oliver, 44.
6 "Praise Song," Barbara Crooker, 45.
7 "Untitled," Kabir (translation by Robert Bly), 52.
8 "Sweet Darkness," David Whyte, 152.
9 "Take Love for Granted," Jack Ridl, 53.
10 "For Calling the Spirit Back from Wandering the Earth in Its Human Feet," Joy Harjo, 189.
11 "The Cure," Albert Huffstickler, 155.
12 "A Community of the Spirit," Rumi (translation by Coleman Barks), 27.
13 "How to Be a Poet," Wendell Berry, 103.
14 "Keeping quiet," Pablo Neruda, 104.
15 "No More Same Old Silly Love Songs," Neil Carpathios, 180.

16 "On How to Pick and Eat Poems," Phyllis Cole-Dai, 21.

17 "Untitled (This is what was bequeathed us)," Gregory Orr, 37.

18 "The Second Music," Annie Lighthart, 36.

19 "Zazen on Ching-t'ing Mountain," Li Po (translation by Sam Hamill), 122.

20 "Savasana: Corpse Pose," Marianne Murphy Zarzana, 125.

21 "You are There," Erica Jong, 123.

22 "Instructions for the Journey," Pat Schneider, 144.

23 "Parallel the Care the Dancer Takes," Hafiz (translation by Daniel Ladinsky), 160.

24 "Love After Love," Derek Walcott, 55.

12-WEEK WORKSHOP CURRICULUM

WEEK 1: THRESHOLD TO PRESENCE

In preparation for today's workshop, read Prompt 2: "Thresholds: Entering a Mindful State" (page 22 in this guide).

Begin the first session with an introduction to the workshop's "Core Principles." Provide an overview of the plan for the workshop. Invite the participants to introduce themselves to begin the process of creating a sense of community. After introductions, invite the participants into five-minutes of silent centering. Conclude the silence with the reading of the opening poem.

Opening Poem: "Bali Hai Calls Mama," Marilyn Nelson, 34.

***Lectio* Poem:** "On How to Pick and Eat Poems," Phyllis Cole-Dai, 21.

Journaling Prompt: Thresholds are all around us: the change of seasons, dawn, dusk, coming home from a long day at work, waking up from a restful sleep. Any of these passages can serve as a threshold into mindful presence. Think about a time when you crossed a threshold. What did you notice? How did it engage your senses? Did you feel your breathing slow down? Did your posture change? How did crossing the threshold change your perspective?

Closing Poem: "blessing the boats," Lucille Clifton, 198.

Before ending for the week, encourage participants to read some of the poems in *Poetry of Presence* before the next class session. Suggest that they begin writing down lines that inspire them so that they can build up a supply for their cento. Remind them that this suggestion is an invitation rather than an assignment.

WEEK 2: EMBRACING BROKENNESS

In preparation for today's workshop, read Prompt 45: "Embracing Brokenness" (page 98 in this guide).

Invite participants into a conversation about the poems they have read in the past week. If they haven't read any, let them know that it's okay, but gently encourage them to do so in the coming week. Then move into five minutes of silent centering.

Introduce the theme of brokenness. What does it mean to embrace brokenness? Invite participants to reflect on this theme during the writing period. It may mean emotional brokenness. It may mean a broken promise. It may mean a broken heirloom that cannot be replaced. Whatever it is, it's personal. Don't be prescriptive. Simply provide the space for each person to explore the theme.

Opening Poem: "Plate," Al Zolynas, 145.

***Lectio* Poem:** "I Will Keep Broken Things," Alice Walker, 146.

Journaling prompt: Think about the broken things in your life. Do you keep them? Are they treasures or debris? Praise something that is broken and examine why it is essential. Is it a literal object? An institution? A part of yourself? Why is it important to embrace it, despite or because of its brokenness?

Closing poem: "The Joins," Chana Bloch, 185.

WEEK 3: EVERYDAY MIRACLES

In preparation for today's session, read Prompt 33: "Everyday Miracles" (page 76 in this guide).

Begin today's session by asking participants to mention something they discovered in a poem during the past week. If anyone has logged lines for their cento, ask them to read one of their choices. This opportunity will provide some examples of how to start thinking about the cento. It will also serve as a gentle reminder for those who haven't begun yet.

Following this conversation, begin the five minutes of Silent Centering.

Opening Poem: "A Little Stone in the Middle of the Road, in Florida," Muriel Rukeyser, 38.

***Lectio* poem:** "Miracle Fair," Wislawa Szymborska (translation by Joanna Trzeciak), 98.

Journaling prompt: What is a miracle? How do you define it? In "Miracle Fair," Szymborska tells us it is a miracle "that so many commonplace miracles happen" (98). Make a list of some common-place miracles you may have missed as you were driving to the supermarket or doing the laundry. Let yourself be surprised and delighted.

Closing Poem: "The Good News," Thich Nhat Hanh, 151.

WEEK 4: THE PARADOX OF JOY

In preparation for today's workshop, read Prompt 19: "The Paradox of Joy" (page 53 in this guide). Acknowledge that joy can be very fraught in these fractious and challenging times. Spend five minutes in Silent Centering.

Opening Poem: "Love after Love," Derek Walcott, 55.

***Lectio* Poem:** "The Word," Tony Hoagland, 41.

Journaling Prompt: In a world torn by crises, joy can seem like an act of disloyalty or denial. We may ask ourselves, "What right do I have to feel joy in a world where suffering runs rampant in the form of hunger, disease, poverty, and injustice?" How do we balance the suffering of the world with our own experience of joy?

Closing Poem: "A Sacrament," Paulann Petersen, 56.

WEEK 5: INSTRUCTIONS FOR LIVING

In preparation for today's session, read Prompt 11: "Instructions for Living" (page 40 in this guide). All of the poems in today's lesson plan take the form of a How-To guide.

Opening Poem: "The Cure for It All," Julia Fehrenbacher, 40.

***Lectio* Poem:** "For Calling the Spirit Back from Wandering the Earth in Its Human Feet," Joy Harjo, 189.

Journaling Prompt: Invite participants to consider their own instructions for living. Ask them to consider what how-to manual they might be looking for. How to breathe? How to laugh? How to cry? Invite them to focus their reflections on the things they most want to teach themselves.

Closing Poem: "Lie Down," Nancy Paddock, 32.

WEEK 6: A BEND IN THE RIVER

To prepare for this week's session, read Prompt 40: "A Bend in the River" (page 89 in this guide). This session is devoted to the old-fashioned notion of going with the flow.

Opening Poem: "Fluent," John O'Donohue, 82.

Lectio **Poem:** "Midlife" Julie Cadwallader Staub, 83.

Journaling Prompt: Ask participants to consider how they navigate the river of life. How do they trust the current when they literally don't know what's around the bend? Ask them to imagine they are floating on a raft on a smoothly flowing river. How does it feel to surrender? How does it feel to "still say yes?"

Closing Poem: "Afterwards," William Stafford, 64.

WEEK 7: WHAT IS MORE GENEROUS THAN A WINDOW?

To prepare for this week's session, read Prompt 29: "What is More Generous Than a Window?" (page 71 in this guide).

Opening Poem: "At the Teahouse, 6 am," Holly J. Hughes, 176.

Lectio **Poem:** "Twilight," Louise Glück, 143.

Journaling Prompt: Invite the group to imagine that they are looking out a window. It can be a window in their home, a remembered window from the house where they grew up, or the first airplane window they ever looked out. It can even be an imagined window. Ask them to consider what draws them to that particular window. What do they see when they look through it? How does the view change? What mood does it call up? What do they hope to see when they look out?

Closing Poem: "Thinking," Danusha Laméris, 47.

WEEK 8: WHAT COMES FROM SILENCE

To prepare for this week's session, read Prompt 6: "What Comes from Silence" (page 30 in this guide). Urge participants to be especially attentive during the Silent Centering. Highlight Wendell Berry's suggestion to "Accept what comes from silence."

Opening Poem: "How to Be a Poet," Wendell Berry, 103.

Lectio **Poem:** "Keeping quiet," Pablo Neruda, 104.

Journaling Prompt: Neruda says, "perhaps a huge silence/might interrupt this sadness/of never understanding ourselves" (104). Ask the group to consider that "huge silence." Encourage them to observe how they experienced the silence of the opening of today's session. Ask them to pay attention to the thoughts that emerged. Encourage them not to push down the thoughts, but rather to welcome them and to observe quite literally how the silence helps them to understand themselves.

Closing Poem: "In the Early Evening," Kirsten Dierking, 196.

WEEK 9: OVERCOMING ANXIETY

To prepare for this week's session, read Prompt 37: "Overcoming Anxiety" (page 83 in this guide). Conscious breathing is considered one of the most effective means of reducing anxiety. Supplement this week's Silent Centering session with a five-minute breathing meditation. There are many approaches to conscious breathing.

Play this video (https://bit.ly/3vPvDAv) of a five-minute breathing exercise.

Opening Poem: "Thinking," Danusha Laméris, 47.

***Lectio* Poem:** "Trough," Judy Sorum Brown, 128.

Journaling Prompt: Ask participants to observe the effect of conscious breathing as a threshold between anxiety and calm. Invite them to consider how (or if) the breathing exercise affected their experience of the poems. Ask them if they can think of a time when pausing to breathe helped lift them out of "the trough."

Closing Poem: "Seas," Juan Ramón Jiménez (translation by Robert Bly), 197.

WEEK 10: POETRY POTLUCK

In preparation for the Poetry Potluck described below, invite participants to choose a poem to share with the group. Don't worry if two people pick the same poem. Their reasons for choosing it will be different, and an interesting conversation always ensues.

Format: Each member of the group reads a poem that they have selected from *Poetry of Presence*. The reader provides the title, author, and page number. Participants write down the page number so they can refer back to the poems during the next step. Allow a minute for reflection between poems. After each person has read a poem, invite the participants to select one poem to explore in depth.

Lectio: Participants silently reread the poem they have selected. Allow five minutes for silent contemplation. Then begin the timed writing period. Allow fifteen minutes and then check-in with the group to see if they want/need more time.

Sharing: Invite participants to offer their reflections beginning with why they chose that particular poem.

WEEK 11: HOW TO WRITE A CENTO

In preparation for the final week of the workshop, engage the group in a practice exercise to help them create their cento. This exercise breaks down any lingering anxiety about the process and also generates excitement about opportunities that await.

Remind the participants about "Elements of a Cento." In this workshop, each line must come from a different poem in *Poetry of Presence.*

Opening Poem: "Instructions," Sheri Hostetler, 90.

This poem echoes the theme of the cento process and the workshop as a whole. How do we pare down to the essentials? How do we decide what we want or need to carry with us? I think of a cento as a very portable anthology. Hostetler's poem provides a blueprint for prioritizing the essentials, which is a good place to start.

Generate a Collaborative Cento. After reading and reflecting on Hostetler's poem, invite participants to take 10 minutes to look through *Poetry of Presence* and choose one line that speaks to them in a particularly meaningful way. Ask them to write down the line, followed by the title, author, and page number. If the group is small, ask them to choose two lines each. You want to have a minimum of 10 lines to work with.

In no particular order, write the lines on the board or in the Screen-Share White Board feature if working in Zoom. Invariably, the random assortment of lines will take on an interesting shape, as demonstrated in the sample below. Some lines will flow together seamlessly. Some will feel out of sync. That's fine. The lines are reorganized in the next step.

Read the random cento aloud. Ask the participants what they think of it. How did it feel to create it together?

Next, leave the lines up on the board and ask each member of the group to arrange them into a new sequence to create his or her own version of the cento. Give them 10 minutes. After everyone is finished, invite them to read their new versions aloud.

* * *

Another approach to this activity is to ask each participant to choose three or four lines from different poems. This will yield a larger pool of lines to work with. Aim for a pool of 20-30 lines.

When you ask the group to organize their own centos, ask them to use no more than 12 lines from the original group. This will give them practice in selecting the lines that work best for their vision of the finished product. This step also provides greater variety when the poems are read aloud to the group.

Once the group has engaged in this project, it eliminates much of the trepidation and elevates the enthusiasm for creating their own centos.

* * *

Here is a sample of a collaborative cento created during a recent workshop:

i reached to love them all

(a cento composed of lines from poems in *Poetry of Presence,* by the
Poetry of Presence Workshop, Summer, 2020)

Let cold water run between your fingers.
You are neither here nor there.
Be grateful even for the boredom that sometimes seems to
    involve the whole world.
The dream of sky requires no passport.
To be steady as a rock and always trembling.
Turn me into song; sing me awake.
Give wine, give bread, give back your heart.
They stitch up the sky, and it is whole again.
I will keep myself.
We'll lose her. Someday each other.

GLOSS: "I REACHED TO LOVE THEM ALL"

Cole-Dai, Phyllis, and Ruby R. Wilson, eds. *Poetry of Presence: An
Anthology of Mindfulness Poems.* Grayson Books, 2017. Print.

Title "Winter Poem," Nikki Giovanni, 94.

1 "Instructions for the Journey," Pat Schneider, 144.
2 "Postscript," Seamus Heaney, 101.
3 "Love for Other Things," Tom Hennen, 76.
4 "We Are of a Tribe," Alberto Ríos, 51.
5 "Trees," Howard Nemerov, 174.
6 "Untitled," Gregory Orr, 37.
7 "Love After Love," Derek Walcott, 55.
8 "Sometimes, I Am Startled Out of Myself," Barbara Crooker,
165.
9 "I Will Keep Broken Things," Alice Walker, 146.

10 "Savasana: Corpse Pose," Marianne Murphy Zarzana, 125.

After reviewing this version, each participant reordered the lines to create his or her own cento. Participants then read their revised versions. The new arrangements of lines yielded remarkable variety in focus and structure. More importantly, the process gave each person confidence to create a cento from scratch.

WEEK 12: A CELEBRATION OF CENTOS

Opening Poem: "Praise Song," Barbara Crooker, 45. This poem sets the tone for a celebration of the time the group has spent together over the past 12 weeks.

The Centos: The final session is devoted to reading the centos that members of the class have written. Each participant reads his or her cento and tells the group what poems the lines came from. If the group is meeting in person, ask each participant to bring enough copies for everyone. If it is on Zoom, enable each participant to share the screen so that the group can read along. Even on Zoom this collective sharing has the effect of a party.

After everyone has read their poems, allow time for conversation about the process.

Invite the class to reflect on a word or phrase that sums up their feeling about the workshop. It can be a line from their cento or from someone else's work. This process helps synthesize the group experience.

Closing Poem: "Gracias/Grace," Rafael Jesús González, 118/119.

If you or someone in the class speaks Spanish, invite them to read "Gracias" (118). It's okay if the listeners don't understand the language. They can still listen and enjoy the music of the poem. The English version, while not a direct translation, complements the Spanish version, conveying an equally comprehensive expression of gratitude. This pair of poems is a wonderful expression of thanks to all the participants for the role each has played in creating the workshop.

SUBJECT INDEX

This index is designed with readers, writers, and workshop facilitators in mind. The subjects are arranged alphabetically followed by the titles of related poems, author names, and the pages on which you can find them in *Poetry of Presence*.

Think of this index as a menu designed to help satisfy a wide variety of appetites. If you are a reader with a hunger for poems about a specific topic, just scroll through the headings to see what will satisfy your craving. If you are trying to write a poem about a specific emotion or theme, you can savor the words of other poets who have tackled similar subjects in their own words. If you are a facilitator looking for poems that will help you whip up new prompts, this index will help you easily locate the ingredients that will entice your workshop participants.

This index can also satisfy the desire to feed others. When you are trying to find the right words to comfort a friend who is grieving or celebrate the joy of being with a loved one, this index can help you find poems that can nourish their hearts.

In "On How to Pick and Eat Poems" Phyllis Cole-Dai says, "Eating one poem can save you, if you're hungry enough" (21). This menu offers a feast to help you satisfy that hunger. *Bon Appetit!*

GRATITUDE
"Praise Song," Barbara Crooker, 45.
"A Poem for My Daughter," Teddy Macker, 113.
"Gracias/Grace," Rafael Jesús González, 118/119.
"I Will Keep Broken Things," Alice Walker, 146.

GRIEF
"Prayer for the Dead," Stuart Kestenbaum, 61.
"For the Sake of Strangers," Dorianne Laux, 153.
"The Thing Is," Ellen Bass, 154.
"The Cure," Albert Huffstickler, 155.
"On Pain," Kahlil Gibran, 184.

IMPERFECTION
"A Poem for My Daughter," Teddy Macker, 113.
"The Joins," Chana Bloch, 185.

INSECT
"A Sacrament," Paulann Petersen, 56.
"Love for Other Things," Tom Hennen, 76.
"The Mosquito Among the Raindrops," Teddy Macker, 92.
"Earthworms," Lynn Ungar, 112.
"Moth Koan," Richard Schiffman, 175.
"Mimesis," Fady Joudah, 192.

INSTRUCTION FOR LIVING
"On How to Pick and Eat Poems," Phyllis Cole-Dai, 21.
"A Community of the Spirit," Rumi (translation by Coleman Barks), 27.
"Lie Down," Nancy Paddock, 32.
"The Cure for It All," Julia Fehrenbacher, 40.
"The Quiet Listeners," Laura Foley, 48.
"Lost," David Wagoner, 49.
"Take Love for Granted," Jack Ridl, 53.
"Instructions," Sheri Hostetler, 90.
"Flowering," Linda Buckmaster, 133.

MUSIC
"The Second Music," Annie Lighthart, 36.
"Untitled (This is what was bequeathed us)," Gregory Orr, 37.
"Versions of Ghalib: Ghazal I," Ghalib (translation by Ruth L. Schwartz), 85.
"My Father at the Piano," Mary O'Connor, 159.
"Parallel the Care the Dancer Takes," Hafiz (translation by Daniel Ladinsky), 160.

NOW
"The Way It Is," Lynn Ungar, 31.
"Sunday Afternoon," Nancy Ann Schaefer, 43.
"Lost," David Wagoner, 49.
"This Morning," David Budbill, 57.
"A Momentary Creed," W. S. Merwin, 87.
"Zazen on Ching-t'ing Mountain," Li Po (translation by Sam Hamill), 122.
"Burning the Journals," Robyn Sarah, 132.
"Instructions for the Journey," Pat Schneider, 144.
"The Moment," Marie Howe, 178.

OBJECT
"Sifter," Naomi Shihab Nye, 30.
"The Patience of Ordinary Things," Pat Schneider, 33.
"In the Middle," Barbara Crooker, 58.
"Burning the Journals," Robyn Sarah, 132.
"Meeting the Light Completely," Jane Hirshfield, 140.
"Plate," Al Zolynas, 145.
"I Will Keep Broken Things," Alice Walker, 146.

ODE
"Sifter," Naomi Shihab Nye, 30.
"Meditation on a Grapefruit," Craig Arnold, 39.
"Love for Other Things," Tom Hennen, 76.
"Earthworms," Lynn Ungar, 112.

SACRED

SILENCE

SKY

SPRING

SUMMER

ABOUT THE AUTHOR

Gloria Heffernan is the author of the poetry collection *What the Gratitude List Said to the Bucket List* (New York Quarterly Books), and the chapbooks *Hail to the Symptom* (Moonstone Press) and *Some of Our Parts* (Finishing Line Press). Her work has appeared in over 70 journals including *Anchor, Chautauqua, Magma (UK), Southword (Ireland), Stone Canoe, Columbia Review,* and *The Healing Muse.*

She holds an M.A. from New York University and teaches at Le Moyne College and the YMCA's Downtown Writers Center in Syracuse, New York.

Gloria lives in Syracuse, New York, with her husband, best friend and first reader, Jim Heffernan.

To schedule a workshop or poetry retreat, contact Gloria:

gloriac225@msn.com
https://gloriaheffernan.wordpress.com

ACKNOWLEDGMENTS

Writing this book has been a daily practice of gratitude-in-action. In the spirit of *Poetry of Presence,* I am mindful of the huge debt I owe to those who have supported and encouraged me in this project:

I am so grateful to Phyllis Cole-Dai and Ruby R. Wilson for inviting me to write this guide, and more importantly for creating the anthology that has inspired me from the very first time I laid eyes on that graceful egret taking a bow on the front cover of *Poetry of Presence.*

I am grateful to Ginny Connors and her team at Grayson Books for recognizing the value and importance of *Poetry of Presence* and for making it available to readers.

I am grateful to Phil Memmer, Executive Director, and Georgia Popoff, Workshop Coordinator, of the Downtown Writers Center who said yes when I proposed the workshop upon which this book is based. They kept the Syracuse YMCA's writing program going throughout the pandemic. Their creativity in a time of crisis provided a lifeline to people who were hungry for community and self-expression in the midst of unprecedented isolation. They welcomed an idea that was a direct response to that hunger.

I am grateful to the generous and creative individuals who

participated in those first workshops: Antoinette Brim-Bell, Judy Carr, Claudia Chang, Sally Gould, Wendy Harris, Victoria Hill-Gilbert, Mei Tow Lam, Bob Sackel, Mary Sieminski, Louisa Stone, and Ren Van Meenen.

I am grateful to the extraordinary women of the "Poetry as a Spiritual Practice Workshop" at Trinity Episcopal Church in Fayetteville, New York: Sr. Laura Bufano, Judy Carr, Sue Cenci, Sue Gibson, Marie Jerge, Alice Irwin, Sue Merchant, Sylvia O'Connor.

I am grateful to Alice Irwin, who painstakingly proofread the manuscript with unfailing patience and precision.

And, as always, I am especially grateful to my beloved husband, Dr. Jim Heffernan, whose constant encouragement and support are nothing short of miraculous. There is no one with whom I would rather shelter-in-place!